The Church Musicians' Handbook

edited by
Sally Trethewey & Rosalie Milne

St Matthias Press
London • Sydney

The Church Musicians' Handbook
© St Matthias Press, 1994

St Matthias Press
PO Box 665
London SW20 8RL
Tel: 081-947 5686

The articles "The key to church music" and "Choosing songs" previously published in *The Briefing, #112*, a periodical published by St Matthias Press.

ISBN 1 873166 05 2

Cover design by Richard Knight

Printed and bound in Great Britain by Redwood Books, Trowbridge, Wiltshire

Contents

Foreword

Music in the church can be an uncredited background or an unpredictable flash point. It sparks off strong feelings and warm words - whether or not we are expert in its skills, and whether it adorns or obscures the gospel of Jesus Christ. Praying musicians who care about the congregation are of immense service to that gospel.

Of all the varied churches I have served, there is none whose music and singing would not be enriched, refreshed or rescued by a thoroughgoing use of this book. Many readers will wish they had seen it earlier.

There has been a relentless wave of new words and music during the past thirty years, much of which has, mercifully, trickled into the sand. But we have also been delightedly discovering great treasures for our own generation and beyond; some is appreciated only in time, and we have much to learn from one another about true values and lasting beauties. Different continents, languages and Christian traditions are becoming aware of one another's modes of worship in order to listen more fully to the word of God.

I am confident that all who want to sing and make music with both their spirit and their understanding will enjoy the bracing Biblical clarity of this practical guide.

Christopher Idle
March 1994

About this handbook

What should distinguish the musician who is a Christian, from other musicians? Is there such a thing as 'spiritual' or 'unspiritual' music? What do people mean when they use the terms 'worship' and 'praise'? Why does the area of music in the church seem to cause so much conflict, when it has the potential to be so effective and helpful? Why do we seem to have so much trouble providing new Christian music which is both biblically based and musically appealing?

These are the sorts of questions that face all Christian musicians and which this handbook seeks to address. Music has potential for teaching and encouraging believers and reaching unbelievers, and can draw the head and heart together. Used wisely, it is a valuable tool. Used unwisely, like any gift, it can cause significant difficulties.

In the following pages, you'll find a variety of material aimed to help you, the church musician, to understand how music should fit in to your church, as well as a wealth of practical advice about making the music in your church work better. Like much church music, this handbook has four parts:

1. **Music and church**

   Three chapters on what the Bible says about music and about how we can use it effectively in our churches.

2. **Bible studies**

   Two studies which consolidate and build on the material in Part 1. These two studies are designed for your music team to work through. They might form part of a day seminar for the musicians in your church.

3. **Practicalities**

A series of short helpful chapters giving practical advice on everything from songleading to running a music team to driving the PA.

4. **Checklists**

A set of four handy checklists that you can take with you to rehearsals or keep by when you're choosing songs.

Much of the material in this handbook sprang from a series of seminars originally given at a Christian youth convention. Our goals for this handbook are the same as for those original seminars: to promote a biblical understanding of the use of music in church, to encourage Christian musicians to use their gifts thoughtfully and lovingly, and to provide practical help for church musicians in doing their job better.

We pray that God will use this handbook to assist you in achieving these goals in your church.

Rosalie Milne and Sally Trethewey

Contributors

Robin Booker is Managing Director of Christian Copyright Licensing.

Nicky Chiswell is a veteran of many church 'items' and has recently released an evangelistic album, *Speechless*.

Greg Clarke is an editor at St Matthias Press who'd be just as happy playing bass guitar.

Rosalie Milne has been involved in music in Christian contexts for most of her life. She chaired the Katoomba Christian Convention music committee for a number of years, during which time the music seminars forming the basis of this handbook were conducted.

Tony Payne has been a church music director and sometime dabbler in composing congregational songs. He is also an editor at St Matthias Press.

David Peterson lectures in New Testament and Christian ministry at Moore Theological College in Sydney. His recent book, *Engaging with God*, offers a biblical theology of worship.

Rob Smith is well-known for his 'Bethlehem' albums (*Our God Reigns* and *Behold Your King)*. He works on the pastoral team at Christ Church, St Ives, in Sydney and currently chairs the KCC music comittee.

Sally Trethewey has worked as a professional musician and led music in Christian meetings for many years. Recently, she released *The Perfect View*, a CD of songs she has written for congregational use.

Dallas Watts is a classically trained singer who teaches drama. He is a regular item singer and songleader.

Steve Williams has worked with musicians' sound systems in churches and conventions for the last twenty years.

John Woodhouse is the Rector of Christ Church, St Ives, in Sydney, and lectures part-time at Moore Theological College.

Part I :
Music and church

Three chapters on what the
Bible says about music and
about how we can use it
effectively in our churches.

The key to church music

1

by John Woodhouse

As far as we can tell, music has always had a place in the lives of Christians, particularly in our corporate experience as the people of God. There is a wealth of evidence for this in the Old Testament; it is not so obvious in the New Testament, but passages such as Ephesians 5 and Colossians 3 suggest that singing was part of normal Christian activity. Today, music still has a place in most Christian gatherings.

A clash of cultures

Although music has always been part of Christian experience, music itself cannot be Christian or non-Christian. There is no such thing as 'sacred music'. Words can be Christian, but not tunes. Singing Latin motets does not make them holy, nor does adding a flute to a heavy metal group. Music is one of those aspects of creation which God gives generously to all humanity. Like money or sex, it is something which sinners pervert by not acknowledging their creator and believers accept with thanksgiving.

But music is also a human art form. As such, it has developed conventions, meanings and values. The resulting 'music culture' affects anyone who is interested in playing or listening to music. The music culture should not call the tune in Christian meetings. Where it is in conflict with gospel principles—and it often is—it must be overruled. This means that church musicians often face a dilemma in working out how and why they serve the church.

One example of this conflict is between *music as performance* and *music as service*. Part of every musician's training is how to perform, how to attract attention and sustain it and how to differentiate oneself from other musicians. However, a Christian is obliged to serve others and this always involves being humble and often requires being inconspicuous. The very things that might enhance music as performance can diminish its value as service. Conversely, being an effective servant may mean making your music less impressive.

On the whole, musicians are greatly appreciated in Christian meetings, because of the enormous enjoyment which people get from singing and listening to music. In fact, for better or worse (and I think the latter), how much people enjoy a Christian meeting is often determined by whether or not they like the music. This places a certain amount of power in the hands of musicians in church. They have the potential to serve the congregation well, but they can also cause great disruption if musical agendas replace the agenda of the gospel. A talented musician whose thinking and conduct is shaped by the gospel is a great asset to any congregation, but a talented musician who is not gospel-directed is, frankly, a pain in the neck.

Christians must not submit to the conventions of any pagan culture. It is of utmost importance that our thinking is transformed by the gospel renewing our minds so that we are no longer conformed to the pattern of the prevailing music culture.

A theology of music?

Although there are many references to music in the Bible (especially in the Psalms), music (as such) is never discussed. It is difficult to imagine a 'theology of music' based on the Bible. It would be like having a 'theology of mathematics' just because the Bible contains numbers.

Our concern is not to have some distinctively Christian understanding of *music*, but to appreciate the *function* of music when Christians meet together. The key to this is the nature and purpose of the Christian assembly.

Why Christians meet

One of the major problems facing Christian churches is our vagueness and uncertainty about why we meet together. We continue to meet because we have always done so and we continue to sing and pray and read the Bible because we would not know what else to do. But we have lost sight of the reasons for doing these things.

Normally, when a group of people meets, the reasons for doing so determine the group's nature and functions. People gather in a movie theatre to watch a movie, or at a bus stop to catch a bus or on a rugby field to kill each other. Sometimes the corporate nature of the event is incidental to its function, such as movie-watching, and sometimes it is essential, such as playing rugby.

We need to seriously ask ourselves this question: what type of gathering is church?

We can do many of our church activities—prayer, learning, reading the Bible—just as well, if not better, alone. The reason for Christians gathering together is not obvious until we understand the nature of the God who gathers us.

The gathering God

The Bible's teaching about why believers meet together is rooted deeply within the nature of God's activity in the world. The nation of Israel knew God as a 'gatherer'. The foundational event of the exodus is remembered as the time that God brought the nation of Israel from Egypt and gathered them at Mount Sinai on the "day of the assembly", to hear his words of instruction (see Ex 19: 1-6; Deut 4: 10). In the promised land, the temple became the symbol of God's presence where God's people would continue to gather together.

But the Old Testament is a record of Israel's disobedience and subsequent judgement by God. This judgement involved scattering the Israelites:

> The LORD said, "It is because they have forsaken my law, which I set before them; they have not obeyed me or followed my law. Instead, they have followed the stubbornness of their hearts; they have followed the Baals, as their fathers taught them." Therefore, this is what the LORD Almighty, the God of Israel, says: "See, I will make this people eat bitter food and drink poisoned water. I will scatter them among nations that neither they nor their fathers have known, and I will pursue them with the sword until I have destroyed them."
>
> Jer 9: 13-16
> (see also Lev 26: 27, 33; Jer 18: 13-17; Ezek 12: 15)

Notwithstanding this, the prophets announced that God had not finished with Israel; he would gather them yet again (see Is 11: 12; Jer 31: 8, 10; Ezek 37: 21,22). The gospel fulfils these prophecies and Jesus' ministry is described thus:

> ...he prophesied that Jesus would die for the Jewish nation, and not only for that nation but also for the scattered children of God, to bring them together and make them one.
>
> Jn 11: 52

> He who is not with me is against me, and he who does not gather with me scatters.
>
> Mat 12: 30

One of the major themes of the epistles is the unity which the gospel brings to all believers, drawing them together under Christ in the manner which God intended. The images of the church are corporate ones: the body, the building, the family, a people.

The gospel of the gathering God provides for us a cornerstone for understanding why Christians meet together.

Gathered in heaven

In Hebrews 12, God describes the consequences of his gathering work. Israel was gathered at Mount Sinai (or Zion), but the Christian church is gathered in heaven, in the city of God. We are assembled before God and the Lord Jesus Christ and "thousands upon thousands of angels in joyful assembly". This describes an event which we do not see today, and yet it is happening. Paradoxically, the gospel is at work in the world, creating a family which is in heaven *now*, gathered before the Father.

The whole of Hebrews is addressing this truth: the symbolic and shadowy covenant of Sinai and the ritualistic activity of the Old Testament 'church' has become a reality in the gospel of Christ. We can now "draw near to God" through Jesus' blood.

The presence of Christ

It is a marvellous fact that, by the Spirit of God, what is true of the heavenly meeting is also true of the earthly one. God is with us! As Jesus says in Matthew 18: 20, "For where two or three come together in my name, there I am with them."

The heavenly presence of the Church, gathered before Christ, has consequences for Christians meeting together. We are to "not give up meeting together, as some are in the habit of doing" (Heb 10: 25); we must "consider how we may spur one another on toward love and good deeds" (Heb 10:24); and we should "encourage one another—and all the more" (Heb 10: 25) as the heavenly reality becomes closer and closer to us. Ephesians 4 explains these activities in more practical detail, but the purpose of the earthly gathering can be summarised in the image of unity in 4:16:

> From him [Christ], the whole body, joined and held together by every supporting ligament, grows and builds itself up in love, as each part does its work.

Here is the significance of the Christian meeting. A church is the people that God has, in a particular place, gathered to himself by the gospel of Christ. It cannot be made more or less significant by the building which holds it, the size of the gathering, its formality, its time and day, nor its music.

Three dimensions of church

1. The Word of God

Our understanding of why Christians meet together will shape the activities which take place in church and the manner in which they are carried out. Consider the scene at Mount Sinai as the Israelites received the commandments of God. They understood that they were in God's presence and this affected their priorities. They were not primarily concerned about the choice of trumpet music! Since God was in their midst, what mattered more than anything else was to listen to what he said.

The earliest church meetings followed the pattern of Sinai. In Acts 2:42, the believers "devoted themselves to the apostles' teaching". In his instructions to the Colossians, Paul commands that the Word of Christ dwell in them richly through wise teaching (Col 3:16,17). Hearing the Word of God remains the fundamentally important activity when Christians meet. It is by his Word that he has called us together. If we do nothing else, we must hear the Word of God from the Scriptures, in whatever format—preaching, study, discussion or otherwise—is appropriate to the meeting. This is the first dimension of any Christian meeting.

2. Prayer

The second dimension of church involves our response to the Word of God. Throughout the New Testament, churches are repeatedly exhorted to pray. Having heard from God and understood his character and his plan for us, we recognise our complete dependence upon him and, through prayer, express this dependence in the most humble way possible.

3. Love

We meet as Christians because God has called us to himself. He has accepted each of us and brought us into his presence. We are, therefore, bound to accept one another. In the Christian meeting, the greatest barriers between people are broken down, since God makes no distinction between us. This is one of the great themes of the New Testament. God makes no distinction between male or female, old and young, not even Jew and Gentile. When Christians love one another, we are expressing the power of the gospel. The practice of the fellowship of the gospel is the third dimension of the Christian meeting.

These are the spiritual dimensions of the Christian meeting: hearing God's Word, responding to him in prayer and loving one another. A consideration of the role of music in church, and any other church activities, must take place within these three dimensions. But one question remains before we can address music specifically.

Praise

Most people describe the point at which music and the Christian meeting come together as 'the time of praise' or 'the time of worship'. These pervasive phrases contain two errors. First, they assume that the sole purpose of coming to church is to praise or worship God, and secondly, that the way we praise God is chiefly through our music.

We haven't room here to offer a full exposition of the Bible's doctrine of worship and praise.* However, we have already looked at why we meet together, and it is not specifically to offer something to God, which is what most people mean when they use the word 'worship'. Our church meetings have three dimensions. Two of them could be described as 'vertical' and the other as 'horizontal'—that is, God speaks to us (vertical, from God to us); we respond to God in prayer and thanksgiving (vertical, from us to God); and we love and encourage one another (horizontal). The following diagram captures it:

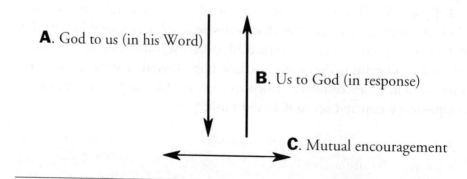

A. God to us (in his Word)

B. Us to God (in response)

C. Mutual encouragement

---

* For a fuller discussion of these issues, see David Peterson's book, *Engaging with God* (Leicester: Apollos, 1992), especially chapter 7 (note the diagram on p 221).

When people say that they come to church to 'worship God' what they usually mean is that the vertical dimension of us offering something to God is the sole or chief reason for coming to church (the B arrow). This is not at all the way that the Bible views church. The purpose of church encompasses all three dimensions: the two verticals and the horizontal. This is why it is confusing and unhelpful to designate our meetings as 'public worship'. It only serves to reinforce a wrong view of church in most peoples' minds, based on a false view of both worship and church. (Music fits into this in that it is often seen as a crucial way for us to offer 'worship' to God, but we will return to this later.)

What is praise?

There is similar confusion regarding praise. We see advertised a 'Service of Prayer and Praise', in which the praise element always refers to singing. In the Christian music industry, a 'praise and worship' album means a collection of devotional songs. All this is a limitation of both praise and music. We need to pay more attention to what the Scriptures mean by the word 'praise'.

The obvious part of the Bible to examine is the book of Psalms. It is very clear here, in almost every psalm, that praise is *declaring what God is like and what he has done*. In general, praise in the psalms is telling others *about* God rather than speaking *to* God. Even in Psalm 105, which is explicitly a psalm of praise to God (see verses 1-2), it is chiefly concerned with telling others about God.

Although the Psalms were undoubtedly sung, they were handed down in Scripture without a note of music attached to them. There are no melody lines in the book of Psalms and yet the element of praise is undeniable. Praising God cannot, therefore, depend upon music. Adding music to the Psalms—a great thing to do—does not increase their 'praise' value.

In the New Testament, the concept of praise remains the same— declaring what God is like and what he has done—but through the gospel, the content of this praise is expanded. We read praises of God at the beginnings of many of the epistles, as the writers remind us of the gospel (see Eph 1; 1 Pet 1). Hebrews 13: 15,16 tells us that God is praised when we acknowledge him and do good in the world:

> Through Jesus, therefore, let us continually offer to God a sacrifice of praise—the fruit of lips that confess his name. And do not forget to do good and to share with others, for with such sacrifices God is pleased.

It is interesting that there is nothing like the book of Psalms in the New Testament. It doesn't have a 'Book of Praises', as the Psalms are called. Rather, the whole New Testament rings with praise, since the highest praise of God is the proclamation of the gospel. The redeemed people of God declare the praises of him who brought them out of darkness into his wonderful light (1 Pet 2:9). Declaring the gospel, whether it be done in song, in preaching, quietly over a cup of coffee or written in a letter, is our praise of God.

Please note—I am not saying we cannot praise God using songs. We can declare his mighty works to one another, and directly to God himself, in a variety of ways, and music is one of them. There is nothing wrong (and everything right) about telling God in song how much we love him and appreciate what he has done for us.

However, I am seeking to correct a pervasive misunderstanding— namely, that praise is only, or even primarily, directed to God and that music is the chief vehicle for such praise.

The place of music

It is absolutely essential that, when we approach the question of the place of music in our meetings, we do so in the light of what church is all about. Otherwise, our conclusions will lead us away from the gospel and away from God. However, with a Biblical understanding of why we meet together as Christians and what we do when we meet, music can be a blessing. Practical advice about church music can be found elsewhere, so I will only offer a few thoughts here.

I want to make three pleas for the consideration of those who are involved in church music.

1. Music must be ministry

'Ministry' is one of the most abused words in Christian jargon. It is often used to refer to one's authority over a particular area of Christian service. "My ministry is my opportunity to use my superior gifts." In this way of thinking, the 'Minister of Music' acts like the 'Minister of Transport', calling the shots for everyone else.

We would do well to rid ourselves of the word 'ministry' and replace it with *serving*, for this is the essence of what Christians must do: serve each other in love. Service is directly opposed to self-promotion and self-satisfaction. Musical talents are valuable to the Christian meeting only if the musicians genuinely desire to serve others. This means more than giving enjoyment to the congregation and it is bound to be in conflict with the performance training that most musicians have undergone at some point.

2. Music needs to be 'demystified'

Music has great power over human beings and that power should not be confused with spiritual experience. In some circles, music has become a barometer of spiritual authenticity. The more you are affected by the 'praise', the more you are in tune with God.

This is unbiblical thinking. The Word of God, prayer and love for one another are the spiritual content of a Christian meeting. None of these three dimensions is made more valuable by music, although each can be well expressed in music. The congregation can, in one voice, sing of God's love or pray together or together read the Word of God out loud. Ephesians 5 and Colossians 3 speak about singing as a means of speaking to one another, as well as to God. Music is not essentially a 'vertical' practice, nor purely a 'horizontal' one. In terms of our diagram above, music needs to be thought of as a useful vehicle for all three dimensions:

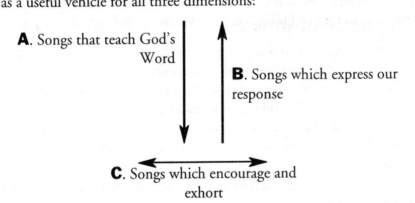

A. Songs that teach God's Word

B. Songs which express our response

C. Songs which encourage and exhort

In other words, music needs to be made less mystical and appreciated for what it is: a good, enjoyable and useful gift of God. Music can be an appropriate way of expressing emotions, just like shouting or laughing. But it should be an expression of the emotions aroused in a believer by the gospel, not by the music.

3. Musicians need to be aware of pitfalls

Finally, a few more words of warning. As this article has suggested at times, the path to serving people through music has its pitfalls. Let me raise two that seem to be widespread in Christian meetings.

1. One of the great experiences of large churches, conferences and rallies

is the mass singing. It lifts the soul to hear a thousand tongues sing to Jesus, just as the hymn says. But this service can become a disservice if, in five years time, all that anyone can remember of the gathering is the great music. We want people to remember how God has changed their minds and lives. If the music serves this end, it is good. If not, we have been betrayed.

2. If you are a songleader, try not to preface songs with comments such as "Let's praise God now". This only confuses people about the meaning of praise and the function of the singing, as if music was the chief or only vehicle of praise. It makes people think that music is the focus of worship.

A godly musician's contribution to a Christian gathering requires more, not less, skill than a musician whose service is not shaped by the gospel. Godly musicians will weigh their contribution against the needs of the church and not their own desires and abilities. And the people of God will benefit from such an orientation. When a musician's heart is set upon hearing God, responding to him and loving one another, his or her service will always be welcome.

Pleasing all the people all the time and other myths

2

by Rob Smith

The aim of this article is both negative and positive. It is negative, since I want to raise and explore some of the difficulties that we encounter—and sometimes create—as we seek to serve God and his people through the use of music. I will deliberately be limiting this discussion to the use of music in our congregational life. You may, of course, belong to a perfect church and be blessed with a perfect group of humble, servant-minded musicians who experience no conflicts or tensions. However, for most of us (all of us, really) things are far from perfect and there are numerous problems which we continually face. It is these that I want to address.

However, my aim is also positive. I hope that through looking at some of these issues and trying to deal with them biblically, we will become clearer in our thinking, more able to see ways ahead, and thus better equipped to continue serving God and his people through the medium of music and song.

Areas of Conflict and Disappointment

There are a number of areas of potential conflict and disappointment which, I suspect, most of us who are involved in Church music would know.

1. Relationships

The first and most important area is that of relationships—most important because life and ministry are really all about relationships. When relationships are strained, life and ministry are likewise strained and it's difficult to function effectively. Let me suggest that there are five different kinds of relationships in most church music groups.

a. The relationships *between the members of the group*. Here there is always the possibility of personal clashes or frustration with those who aren't as competent as others.

b. The relationship *between the group and their leader*. Here there is the possibility of the group being unreliable or the leader being overbearing.

c. The relationship *between the leader and the pastor or ministry team*. Here there is the possibility of a conflict of direction, or disagreement over the role of music, or the possibility of one party feeling threatened by the other.

d. The relationship *between the musicians and the congregation*. Here there may be a lack of appreciation from the congregation or insensitivity on the part of the musicians.

e. The relationship *of the musician to his/her own ego*. I include this because musicians are sometimes very sensitive people (sometimes very proud people, as well) and for this reason can often feel criticism very deeply, or become very disillusioned by their own motives. (Over the years I have spoken to numerous musicians who have felt like dropping out because of disappointment with their own mixed motives.)

2. Musical Tastes

Musical taste is a second major problem area because most people unconsciously (or consciously) think that *their* musical taste is superior to that of others, and therefore believe it *ought* to be catered for. However, the fact is that our likes and dislikes are usually very subjective, despite the pseudo-Christian rationalisations we sometimes find for advocating their superiority. Having said that, I am reasonably convinced that certain styles of music are conducive to church use—but I suspect this conviction is affected by my culture. Be that as it may, many conflicts over music in church ultimately have to do with differences in taste.

3. Purpose and Exposure

A third area of potential conflict has to do with whether the musicians and the minister/pastor agree upon the *purpose* of the music group (and generally of music within the Christian meeting). For instance, in some church meetings the music is right at the centre of what is happening. In others it may play a more subservient role. In various situations I've seen musicians (and ministers)—sometimes rightly, sometimes wrongly—get very frustrated. If, as sometimes happens, a kind of stalemate is reached, there is (sadly) great scope for ungodly forms of manipulation. In one church I heard about, the pastor was told that if he insisted that a particular group of musicians only played every second Sunday, then, as a form of protest, they wouldn't come on the weeks they weren't 'performing'.

These are some of the *areas* of conflict and disappointment which church musicians experience (of course, there are others). What are some of the *causes* behind them?

Causes of Conflict and Disappointment

1. Unrealistic Expectations

Perhaps the biggest cause of problems is *unrealistic expectations* about many areas:

a. About our *church meetings*. Many Christians seem to unconsciously expect a 'heaven now' experience each time they gather. Sometimes, in order to achieve this, they use music to create an atmosphere that transports them into a new dimension of spiritual awareness. Now I'm not saying that we shouldn't find singing an exhilarating experience when we meet together—we should! And, yes, there is a sense in which our joining together in singing praise is both a participation and anticipation of the worship of heaven.[*] But we must remember that we sing *in hope*, for we do *not yet* see God. Likewise we also sing in order to build up each other to live more faithfully *in this world*— not to escape from it. Frankly, it's all too tempting and all too easy to turn congregational singing into a form of escapism in order to try and taste heaven now in a way that is not given to us.

---

[*] See D. G. Peterson, *Engaging with God*. Leicester: Apollos, 1992, p. 277.

b. About *music itself.* Because music is an emotional medium, it can often affect us with great power. Many Christians have been taught to identify the emotions generated by singing with the work of God's Spirit. Thus, music, in some quarters, has come to be seen as the primary vehicle of the Spirit's ministry to us. However, we must be careful at this point, lest we confuse the issues. First, the presence of emotion does not necessarily indicate that the Spirit of God is at work, just as lack of emotion does not mean that he is not at work. Secondly, the Spirit's fundamental and unmistakable ministry is by means of his sword, that is the Word of God (Eph 6:17). The primary (and most direct) forms of this ministry are those of preaching, teaching and the reading of Scripture. Nevertheless, where that Word is being sung (and I don't only mean by singing 'straight Scripture'), then we likewise can be sure that the Spirit of God is doing his work. The evidence of this work will be appropriate repentance and faith in God's promises.

c. About *people's tastes and abilities.* Not everyone likes what you like, nor does everybody necessarily enjoy singing as many (or few!) songs as you do. It doesn't necessarily mean they are unspiritual. I was visiting a church once where they sang so much that I actually wished they would stop—and I love singing! We can also expect our people to be better singers than they really are. Some music is simply too demanding for some congregations to sing. We need to work sensitively with the people whom God has given us and not try to force them to live up to our dream (whatever it might be).

d. About *ourselves and others.* It is again unreal to expect that you (pastor or musician) will be able to *please all of the people all of the time* or to expect that you won't have to compromise your own preferences for the sake of others, and for the sake of the gospel. Above all, it would be naive and arrogant to believe that your way of doing things is always right, or to think that everyone who doesn't agree with you is hindering the work of God! (Unfortunately, I've met this attitude many times). I also suggest that you don't burden your little music group and struggling congregation (if that is what they are) with the expectation that they are going to be able to sound like the latest Christian music tape (even if it's one of mine!).

2. Personal Ambitions

A second and very dangerous source of conflict can be *personal ambition*. For instance, some church musicians are really frustrated rockstars who are looking for a stage on which to perform (so, of course, are some preachers). Having come out of a background of being a very ambitious rock entertainer, I know how tempting it is to try and use a Christian meeting as an opportunity for drawing peoples' praises to yourself. Please don't misunderstand me: I don't think that Christian musicians should be sheepish and mediocre, nor do I have any problem with Christians performing in the right context. But I do believe that when we're singing congregationally, there is a kind of performance which distracts people to such an extent that we are drawn away from what and why we are singing. Often behind that distraction lies the driving ambition of an insecure person with a longing to be noticed and applauded.

Personal ambition can be a major cause of relational conflict, particularly where there is a clash of authority because someone is wrongly striving for power and control. Because ambitious people are usually insecure, they often cannot (or will not) hear what others are saying nor are they usually interested in making friendly compromises. If you recognise some of these traits in yourself, then you need to repent of them, be forgiven for them, talk honestly to someone about them and pray with that person for the furthering of God's transforming work in your life. Churches have been and are being torn apart by such sins!

3. Poor Communication

A third source of trouble is *poor communication*. Often ministers and musicians find themselves at cross-purposes simply because they have failed to take the time to talk to each other and find a way of working together towards the same goal. Sometimes we deliberately keep people in the dark because it gives us a sense of power. But if we are going to work Christianly and effectively, we've got to learn to talk to each other, learn from each other and hear what each other is saying. It may just be, for example, if you are continually running into difficulties with your pastor over the music, that you're going to have to sit down and prayerfully work out why there is a clash of expectations. It can be hard work, but it's rarely a waste of time!

Issues Needing Careful Reflection

There is probably no uniform set of answers or solutions to the problems we have been discussing. Clearly, there is a great need for prayer in all things.

There are, however, a number of issues that we need to get clear if we are going to be able to better serve God and his people in these matters.

1. Leaders and Followers

The first issue has to do with the subject of authority and obedience. Because we live in a democratic, egalitarian age (and because we are inherently rebellious), we often have great trouble coping with authority, both when we are under it and when we are exercising it! But the fact is that in our churches certain people are normally given the responsibility of overseeing what goes on—whether we call them ministers, pastors or elders—and that is a good and godly thing. Some churches even have a music pastor (either part-time or full-time), whose specific job is to oversee the music. In other churches, one person or a number of people may voluntarily fulfil that same role without the official recognition. Whatever the case, there is normally some kind of leadership structure (be it official or functional) in place.

If you are under a leader of some kind, then God desires you to respect that person and to co-operate with them, working within the boundaries they set for you. Things may not be exactly as you think they should be, but so what? Who says your way is best, anyway? By all means, talk to your leaders, share ideas with them, share frustrations with them. But unless you are fully convinced that they are moving in a way that is in opposition to God's revealed will, then support them. The best advice for those who feel restricted is to first prove yourself faithful, trusting that in (God's) time you'll be given the freedom and responsibility you currently desire.

If you are a leader, then lead by all means, but make sure that your leadership works itself out in love and not in a dictatorship. In other words, care for those who are under you, listen to them, talk to them, show them where you believe things should head and what their part is in getting there. Involve them in what is happening, that they might all the time be learning and growing in their capacities and potential to lead and be responsible. Aim to ultimately do yourself out of a job!

2. Service is the Goal

Secondly, understand that whoever you are and whatever responsibility you have, *service* is the goal—not self-promotion or self-protection. At the risk of stating the obvious, in all things our aim as Christians must be nothing else than to serve God by obeying him and to serve others by building them up. If this really is what we are striving for, then we may find that lots of the things we often get steamed up about are not the issues we thought they were. For instance, we may realise that our demand that the music be led a certain way, or that certain types of songs be sung, may in fact be a self-centred thing or purely a thing of taste! Therefore, serving others will inevitably mean that we are free to compromise on all sorts of inconsequential things, so that we can serve our brothers and sisters in the way that is most helpful and appropriate for them.

3. The Priority of the Word

Finally, there is one thing that we ought not to be indifferent about—the priority of the Word of God in our meetings. The reason for this is simple; it is the presence of the Word of God, above all else, which makes a meeting *Christian*. As I have already said, the Word of God can be sung to us, and the songs we sing together *ought* to convey the Word of God to us (if they don't, then we'd better get rid of them and find some that do!). That is why the singing of "psalms, hymns and spiritual songs" (Col 3:16) is an important part of Christians gathering together. But as we saw above, the most direct ways in which the Word of God comes to us are through the reading of the Scriptures, through their exposition in preaching and teaching, and through our speaking of the Truth to one another in conversation. So whil I believe that God means us to enjoy music, to do it well and to appreciate its beauty, and even to use it as a way of addressing him, it must always remain the servant of the spoken Word of God if we are to use it faithfully and fruitfully as we meet together.

What Really Pleases God?

The church musician's ultimate question is this: 'What really pleases God?'. Is it having the best music group in your area, or a computerised over-head set up, or a new sound system in your church? Or (as good as those things might be) is God ultimately more concerned about something else, something much more basic? Let me remind you of some familiar words from the apostle Paul:

> If I speak in the tongues of men and of angels, but have not love, I am only a resounding gong or a clanging cymbal. If I have the gift of prophecy and can fathom all mysteries and all knowledge, and if I have a faith that can move mountains, but have not love, I am nothing. If I give all I possess to the poor and surrender my body to the flames, but have not love, I gain nothing.
>
> 1 Cor 13:1-3

It would truly be a tragedy if, in our desire to have good music in our gatherings, all we ended up with was a fistful of techniques and lacked the most basic thing, that which God himself is said to be: love. For what really excites God is when a group of Christians—musical or tone-deaf—begin to serve one another *in love* and speak the truth to one another *in love*. I honestly can say that it is my sincere hope that all of us will have great music in our churches, that it will be led well and that our musicians will continue to increase in skill and ability. But more than all of that, I hope that we may learn to so live and operate in genuine self-giving love, that the use of all our gifts will be controlled by this love, and that our personal tastes be subordinated to our desire to serve others.

The old and the new

Understanding and using hymns effectively

by David Peterson

3

When the apostle Paul wrote about the use of "psalms, hymns and spiritual songs" (Eph 5:19; Col 3:16), he made no sharp distinction between the different categories. Old Testament psalms and newly coined songs of praise would both have been covered by this expression.

Since apostolic times, Christians have continued to sing the *Psalms* in various forms. *Hymns* have been rather narrowly understood as congregational songs in a regular or metrical form, usually containing more than a single verse. Although a *chorus* is strictly a segment of a hymn that is repeated throughout (e.g. 'Trust and obey...' in the hymn 'When we walk with the Lord'), in modern usage it has often come to mean a short, one-verse song. The term *songs* is generally used to include everything from a solo item or group contribution to a congregational chorus or irregular hymn form.

Like many of the biblical psalms, good Christian hymns or songs will tell us what God is like and what he has done. They will encourage us to respond to him with faith, repentance, love, hope, obedience or gratitude. At the same time, they may actually be the means of making such a response together, there and then. Ideally, they will stimulate an ongoing response to God when the meeting is over and people go back to their homes or places of work. Those planning church services must consider carefully the function of songs at particular stages in the meeting. Is this hymn meant to be a response to the readings or sermon? Is it really a challenge to listen carefully? Is it an invitation to prayer or an expression of thanksgiving?

Words and music: what they achieve

We all know the affective value of music—the way it can touch our emotions and speak to the deep recesses of our personalities. Israel's praise was normally accompanied with instruments to produce a vigorous and loud noise, as an expression of strong emotion (e.g., Ps 150). But music can be manipulative if it is simply used to create a mood or to entertain. When it is used to *highlight the meaning of the words*, it can plant the word of God memorably and powerfully in our hearts.

> Music is a language in its own right, and, as an art, a means of communication. Using pitches, rhythms, harmonies, timbres, and form it is as capable today of running the gamut of emotions from exaltation through gaiety, joy, excitement, solemnity, and fear to extreme dejection and sorrow as it was in the days of the biblical singers—Miriam, David and Zechariah.
>
> A. C. Lovelace & W. C. Rice, *Music and Worship in the Church*
> (Nashville: Abingdon, Rev. ed., 1976), 16.

Music makes it possible for a number of people to exercise their gifts for the edification of the congregation. As instrumentalists join together to accompany the singing, as individuals or groups sing to challenge or encourage the congregation and as the people of God sing together about what they believe, it can be *a particular expression of the unity we have in Christ.*

Unfortunately, many people are used to thinking about music in quite selfish terms. We have such strong feelings about what we like that we are tempted to say, "I am not even willing to listen to your kind of music, let alone sing your songs!". Music is potentially a source of great division in a congregation. It is an area where Christians can be quite unrestrained in expressing their sinfulness! If it is to be a meaningful and effective part of body life, we need to apply the Scriptures quite specifically to this problem area and do so in a public way.

Leaders should encourage members of their congregations to *welcome the contributions of others* (if they are honouring to God and are able to build up the body), following teaching on the variety and use of gifts from passages like Romans 12 and 1 Corinthians 12-14. The other side of this is learning how to *share our insights, preferences and contributions for the benefit of the body* and not just as a means of self expression. Here, as in other areas of ministry, we need to "speak the truth in love", which is essential to the process of edification (see Eph 4:15-16).

In the context of church, *words must take priority over music*, with music serving the proclamation and application of Scriptural truth. If hymn tunes are not well chosen, or if the musical accompaniment is inappropriate, the process of edification may be hindered. Members of the congregation may be so confused or annoyed by the music that they cannot participate meaningfully in the singing. Those responsible for choosing the music must have regard for the sense and intention of the words. They must also take account of the musical tastes, experience and skill of the congregation in view. Questions such as these must be asked: "Is this tune pitched too high at certain points?", "Are the intervals in the melody line too difficult?" or "Does the rhythm vary in a way that unskilled people will not easily follow?".

Balancing the old and the new

The aim in any congregation should be to develop a musical tradition that is appropriate to the group concerned. Of course, many churches have very different congregations meeting at different times in the same building. Each will have particular musical preferences and needs.

However, there are two dangers to be avoided here. Firstly, we can develop *only a narrow musical tradition*, not encouraging people in a particular congregation to broaden their musical horizons. Secondly, we can also become *faddists,* accepting any current popular musical movement as the ultimate answer. Individuals and congregations often want to stick with the familiar and pleasant. "That was good", they say, "let's have it again... and again... and again!" They may like to sing only 'the good old songs' because they are trying to relive some past heart-warming experience (e.g., people who went to Billy Graham crusades are much attached to 'How great thou art'). However, this can also be the attitude to modern songs or choruses that 'do something special' for people. We can be hooked on subjective values and experiences.

If we become the victims of any particular musical trend we will soon be out of date. If we simply respond to the latest fads we will provide people with nothing of permanent value and contribute to the spread of secularism, with its insistence that only 'now' matters. In particular, contemporary

Christians need to be put in touch with *the contributions and insights of former generations of believers*. There is a rich treasury of hymns from across the centuries that can minister to our needs today and provide what is lacking in modern songs or choruses. Of course, the reverse is also true: some modern music expresses biblical truth that is hardly emphasized in older material.

There is always the danger of widening the generation gap and alienating some altogether by restricting the congregation to essentially one type of music.

> All church music should have the ability to speak to the entire congregation. If the music is divisive, if most of the people do not understand what is happening, if it does not have meaning to most, then it is probably improper and wrong.
>
> A. C. Lovelace & W. C. Rice, *Music and Worship in the Church* , 203.

On the other hand, one of the reasons why ministers are often unduly restrictive in the choice of hymns and other songs is that they underestimate the ability of a congregation to learn and appreciate new or more complicated music when it is properly taught.

Rediscovering hymns

Various types of hymns

By virtue of their structure and length, hymns differ from choruses in being able to:

a. *Provide a more extensive treatment of a biblical passage* over a number of verses (e.g., 'Tell out my soul', based on Lk 1:46-55);

b. *Develop a biblical theme*, looking at it from various points of view in different verses (e.g., 'Jesus thy blood and righteousness', exploring the implications of Jesus' death, or 'How sweet the name of Jesus sounds', meditating on the significance of the name of Jesus for believers);

c. *Tell the story of someone else's spiritual pilgrimage* so that we can identify with it (e.g., 'Amazing grace' or 'And can it be?');

d. *Paint a picture of some biblical scene* to encourage us to respond appropriately (e.g., 'My song is love unknown', focussing particularly on the final week of Jesus' life, or 'Jerusalem the golden', portraying the joys of the heavenly city);

e. *Explore the different dimensions of the response we should make to God* (e.g., 'Be thou my vision' or 'Lord of creation to you be all praise').

Hymns through the ages

Hymns have varied in musical style and content throughout the centuries. To a very large extent the words have reflected the theological emphases and concerns of each era. There are particular strengths and weaknesses to be observed in the various types of hymns that we have available from the different periods of church history. (A more detailed and comprehensive treatment of this subject is offered by W. J. Reynolds & M. Price, *A Survey of Christian Hymnody* [Carol Stream Ill.: Hope Publishing, 1987].)

1. The earliest centuries and the medieval period

Most church music in this era was written for sections of the Greek or Latin Mass (e.g., the ancient hymn 'Glory to God in the highest', the Nicene Creed, and various sentences and responses). Congregational involvement would have been limited. In the monasteries, hymn singing in a more metrical or rhythmical form was introduced, but this was only enjoyed by a limited number of people. Many of the early monastic hymns were associated with *times and seasons of the day or year* (e.g., 'O gladsome light' [3rd century] or 'Father we praise you, now the night is over' [6th century] or 'Sing my tongue the glorious battle' [6th century] or 'The Day of resurrection' [8th century]).

2. The Reformation legacy

The hymn as a popular religious lyric, to be sung by the congregation in the regular Sunday gathering, really emerged with the German Reformation. This flowed from the teaching of the Reformers about the priesthood of all believers and their rediscovery of the importance of preaching in the congregation. Hymns became a vehicle for corporately affirming *confidence in God and the gospel*. Some of Martin Luther's own hymns were based on portions of the Psalms (e.g., 'A mighty stronghold', from Ps 46) and others on New Testament texts or themes (e.g., 'Christ lay in death's strong bands', from 1 Cor 5:7-8).

German hymns often have a long metre (a large number of syllables in a line) and many lines to a verse. Strong tunes in a fairly measured and slow beat highlight the sense of confidence and adoration conveyed by the words. A number of early Lutheran pastors were inspired to write hymns which were free compositions, not necessarily tied to Scriptural texts but relating some aspect of biblical truth or Christian experience (e.g., 'Now thank we all our

God', 'O sacred head sore wounded' or 'Jesu, priceless treasure'). J.S. Bach adapted and arranged many Lutheran hymns as chorales for his cantatas, to be sung by soloists and choir in regular Sunday services and on special occasions.

In Geneva, the Book of Psalms became the sole vehicle of the people's musical expression. Rediscovery of the richness of this part of God's Word was one reason for this. Another was the belief that *only strict paraphrases of Scripture were appropriate for use in church.* The Genevan model was followed in different degrees by Anglicans and Presbyterians. The oldest surviving example in English is 'All people that on earth do dwell' (based on Ps 100) by William Kethe (d. 1594). Other early examples include 'Let us with a gladsome mind' (based on Ps 136) by John Milton (1608-74), 'Through all the changing scenes of life' (based on Ps 34) and 'As pants the hart for cooling streams' (based on Ps 42), both by Nahum Tate and Nicholas Brady. (Tate and Brady wrote and revised many metrical psalms and published their collection in 1696. It became a standard hymn book for many years in Anglican churches.)

3. Eighteenth century developments

One of the greatest hymn writers of all time was the Congregationalist minister Isaac Watts (1674-1748). He was concerned that *the Old Testament should be used and interpreted in the light of the New* and that the Psalms in particular should become Christian praises. Thus, Psalm 72 in his metrical Psalter became 'Jesus shall reign where'er the sun'. Apart from his excellent paraphrases of the Psalms (e.g., 'O God, our help in ages past', based on Ps 90), Isaac Watts wrote literally thousands of hymns on 'Divine Subjects', some of which were based on specific passages (e.g., 'Come let us join our cheerful songs', based on Rev 5), and some of which, though unquestionably biblical, were not paraphrases and relied upon no single passage of Scripture (e.g., 'When I survey the wondrous cross'). He was concerned that hymns should express *the thoughts and feelings of those who sang,* as well as proclaiming the eternal truths of Scripture.

Charles Wesley (1707-88) was the most prolific and, some would say, the most gifted of all English hymn writers. He and his brother John encouraged and developed a particular style of hymn singing amongst the Methodists that soon spread to the evangelical party of the Church of England. The Wesleys taught people everywhere to *sing about Christ,* using attractive tunes to match compelling poetry. Their hymns played an important part in the revival that swept England and North America. Charles contributed more than 5,500 hymns and John over 50 to various publications. Both knew the immense importance of hymns for missionary, devotional and instructional purposes. Even more so than Watts, Charles Wesley wrote about *Christian experience* ('And can it be?' is autobiographical). He focussed on the love of God, particularly as seen in the atoning sacrifice of Jesus. Personal faith, holiness and sanctification, Christian fellowship and the Lord's Supper were also dominant themes in his hymns. Charles experimented freely with the hymn form, using up to one hundred different metres in contrast with the more restricted range of Watts. Some of the finest examples of his writing are: 'Christ the Lord is risen today', 'Christ, whose glory fills the skies', 'Jesus lover of my soul', 'Love divine all loves excelling' and 'O for a thousand tongues'.

Another significant milestone in this period was the publication of an evangelical hymnal by John Newton and William Cowper in 1779. These hymns were part of the *religious education programme* instituted in the village of Olney. Cowper's contributions included 'O for a closer walk with God' and 'God moves in a mysterious way', and Newton's 'How sweet the name of Jesus sounds', 'Glorious things of thee are spoken' and 'Amazing Grace'.

4. The nineteenth century

The poetic ideals and literary style of the Romantic Movement, with its focus upon nature, beauty and sentiments, were reflected in the development of hymns in the nineteenth century. Reginald Heber (1783-1826) is regarded as a significant figure in this period. He wrote to persuade the Church of England to use congregational hymns which were inspiring, yet related to *the Bible readings for Sundays and holy days in the Prayer Book Calendar*. His most famous composition is 'Holy, holy, holy! Lord God Almighty!' (for Trinity Sunday). As the Oxford Movement re-introduced Catholic theology and practices into the Church of England, many early Greek and Latin hymns were translated and published.

Other hymn writers of the nineteenth century who reflected the romantic spirit included Charlotte Elliot ('Just as I am, without one plea'), Robert Grant ('O worship the King') and Henry Lyte ('Abide with me'). Although there was a massive outpouring of hymns in the Victorian period, many are too dated in language, music and poetic style to be used today. Well-known survivors include 'The church's one foundation', 'For all the saints', 'Crown him with many crowns', and 'Take my life and let it be'.

5. The twentieth century

Developments in this century have been complex. Hymns in a traditional style continue to be written, but with contemporary language and more modern musical forms (e.g., 'Tell out my soul', 'Lord Jesus Christ', and 'Lord for the years'). Modern tunes have been written for old words (e.g., Ralph Vaughan Williams' version of 'Come down, O love divine' and 'For all the saints'; Geoffrey Beaumont's versions of 'O Jesus I have promised' and 'Now Thank we all our God'). Various attempts to put the Psalms into a singable form are reflected in *Psalm for Today*, *Songs from the Psalms* and their predecessors.

The Charismatic Movement, with its emphasis on the work of the Holy Spirit, has generated an international movement of song writing. This tradition tends to focus on *congregational life and ministry*, rather than on the Spirit's work in evangelism or in promoting holiness and spiritual maturity. Simplicity and variety of style are the characteristics of material in a book like *Songs of Fellowship*.

Rhythms and harmonies in contemporary Christian music are much influenced by folk, rock and jazz idioms. Traditional metrical forms are not often followed. Sometimes the lyrics are confused and meandering, lacking theological depth and substance. Repetition is often used to create a mood. In the *Scripture in Song* tradition biblical verses and phrases are used extensively, but sometimes obscurely (e.g., 'Let there be a canopy stretched forth to thy praise'). There is a bright and vigorous note of celebration in much of this material but little to compare with the doctrinal strength of older hymns. Insufficient attention is given to the great gospel events and their meaning for us all. Important biblical themes such as suffering and judgment are largely neglected in contemporary Christian music. Perhaps one of our problems is that the words are often written by musicians instead of pastors and teachers. Where are the Luthers, the Watts, the Newtons and the Wesleys of today? We need more authors who are theologically astute and have a way with words.

Modern music is not always easy to sing. Sometimes there are difficult time changes, syncopated sections or unusual intervals to be learned (e.g., 'Blessed is the man' from *Psalm Praise*). More care and preparation may be needed to teach some items to a congregation. Occasionally the words in one verse of a song may not fit the tune as well as those in another verse! Above all, in assessing the vast array of contemporary songs, *content* will have to be considered. In this task, comparison with the achievements of former generations is extremely helpful.

Conclusion

There have been some exciting and creative contributions to the treasure house of Christian music in recent decades. But it would be foolish to sing only modern songs and abandon some of the riches we have inherited. Church services should, in my opinion, regularly contain a couple of traditional hymns as well as a mix of contemporary songs. To help people understand and appreciate hymns, something of their meaning or of the author's background could be briefly conveyed to the congregation. (Service leaders would find help from books such as C. Idle, *Well-loved Hymns and their Stories* [Lion: Oxford, 1989] E. Houghton, *Christian Hymn Writers* [Evangelical Press of Wales, 1982] and F. Colquhoun, *A Hymn Companion* [Hodder: London, 1985].) The tunes may need to be taught to those who are unfamiliar with them. In the final analysis, a hymn that is well written and appropriately placed in the flow of a service will commend itself to people of all ages and unite them as they fulfil the words of Ephesians 5:18-20:

> Do not get drunk on wine, which leads to debauchery. Instead, be filled with the Spirit, speaking to one another with psalms, hymns and spiritual songs, singing and making melody in your heart to the Lord, always giving thanks to God the Father for everything, in the name of our Lord Jesus Christ.

Part II
Studies

Two studies designed for you
and your music team.

The following two studies are intended to draw
upon both the biblical passages cited and the ideas
discussed in the chapters at the beginning of this
handbook. Although they can be used by individuals, they are designed to be discussed by a group of
musicians as part of preparation for being involved
in music in church.

There are two studies; each can be covered in
around one hour. Ideally, they should be covered
in two separate sessions, giving sufficient time to
discuss the issues raised and think about the implications of what the Scriptures teach. They will be
most profitable if one or two people have read the
studies beforehand and can guide the group
through the questions.

Music in the Bible 4

by Greg Clarke

The purpose of church

In Hebrews 10:25, Christians are encouraged to continue meeting together. Some of our churches have so many different gatherings—Sunday services, Bible study groups, prayer cells, men's breakfasts—that we seem to have misread the verse as 'meet together continually'. But why do we do what we do in these gatherings? Unfortunately, we don't always know why. We just do it. And the longer we continue to meet without being sure of our objectives in doing so, the easier it becomes to misunderstand what church is all about.

Think it Through

1. Why should Christians meet together as a church? (You might like to refer back to Chapter One by John Woodhouse.)

2. What are some common misunderstandings about the purpose of church?

3. Describe, in as much detail as possible, your ideal church service.

The Bible has a lot to say about what we should do in church and how we should do it. God also reveals the purpose behind the commands he gives us for our meetings together.

Investigate

READ EPHESIANS 4:1-16 (reprinted below)

As a prisoner for the Lord, then, I urge you to live a life worthy of the calling you have received. Be completely humble and gentle; be patient, bearing with one another in love. Make every effort to keep the unity of the Spirit through the bond of peace. There is one body and one Spirit—just as you were called to one hope when you were called—one Lord, one faith, one baptism; one God and Father of all, who is over all and through all and in all.

But to each one of us grace has been given as Christ apportioned it. This is why it says: "When he ascended on high, he led captives in his train and gave gifts to men." (What does "he ascended" mean except that he also descended to the lower, earthly regions? He who descended is the very one who ascended higher than all the heavens, in order to fill the whole universe.)

It was he who gave some to be apostles, some to be prophets, some to be evangelists, and some to be pastors and teachers, to prepare God's people for works of service, so that the body of Christ may be built up until we all reach unity in the faith and in the knowledge of the Son of God and become mature, attaining to the whole measure of the fullness of Christ.

Then we will no longer be infants, tossed back and forth by the waves, and blown here and there by every wind of teaching and by the cunning and craftiness of men in their deceitful scheming. Instead, speaking the truth in love, we will in all things grow up into him who is the Head, that is, Christ. From him the whole body, joined and held together by every supporting ligament, grows and builds itself up in love, as each part does its work.

1. List the characteristics of a good church.

2. What is God's purpose in giving Christians different responsibilities and gifts (v.11-13)?

Think it Through

Here is a list of activities which often take place at church. Organize them in order of importance to the church meeting and explain your ordering. Discuss any differences in ranking.

prayer	The Lord's Supper
singing	preaching
reading the Bible	church news
musical items	saying creeds
eating together	money collection

(add other activities that happen at your church)

Using gifts

The issue of gifts is one which can cause great division among Christians. Some people see gifts as something to keep to ourselves; some are keen to share them; others want to show them off to anyone who is within range. The key to using gifts is understanding why they are given. This is important to us in considering the use of our musical gifts in church.

Investigate

READ COLOSSIANS 3:12-17 (reprinted below)

Therefore, as God's chosen people, holy and dearly loved, clothe yourselves with compassion, kindness, humility, gentleness and patience. Bear with each other and forgive whatever grievances you may have against one another. Forgive as the Lord forgave you. And over all these virtues put on love, which binds them all together in perfect unity.

Let the peace of Christ rule in your hearts, since as members of one body you were called to peace. And be thankful. Let the word of Christ dwell in you richly as you teach and admonish one another with all wisdom, and as you sing psalms, hymns and spiritual songs with gratitude in your hearts to God. And whatever you do, whether in word or deed, do it all in the name of the Lord Jesus, giving thanks to God the Father through him.

1. How are members of the church to treat each other?

2. What reasons does the passage give about why we should do this?

3. What are the purposes of music? (See also 1 Cor 14:26 —" What then shall we say, brothers? When you come together, everyone has a hymn, or a word of instruction, a revelation, a tongue or an interpretation. All of these must be done for the strengthening of the church.")

4. How is singing related to the "word of Christ"?

5. Is it especially hard for musicians to "clothe themselves with humility"? If so, why?

6. How might musicians especially express love and service to others?

Think it Through

1. How can we make sure that our music in church achieves these goals? What aspects of the music facilitate this? What things hamper it?

2. Discuss this statement: "God has given me the gift of playing the guitar. I will be going against his will if I don't play in church. If I stop playing, he might take the gift away from me."

3. Talk about what it means, in practical terms, to have right relationships with:

- your music leader

- your church leader

- the other musicians

- the congregation

4. How far will you go in loving others and being their servant?

- playing songs you don't like?
- being happy not to play?
- being happy not to play a song that you've diligently rehearsed when the meeting runs over time?
- being on time to rehearsals?

List other practical examples of servanthood. Talk about how to overcome the biggest obstacles to humble, loving service as a musician.

Further optional study: Bible word search

The following word search is optional, but we've included it for those who would like to go into a little more depth. You would need to allow a separate session, or you may like to complete the work privately and then come together to discuss your findings.

Investigate

Look up all of the references listed and put a tick in the table of purposes (a reference may fit into more than one category of purpose). Don't spend too long on each reference.

You will notice immediately that the majority of the references are from the Old Testament, in particular the book of Psalms. Be careful in your analysis of these verses to take note of where they occur in the Bible, how this affects their meaning and which passages seem to be of most significance to developing an understanding of what the Bible has to say about music in church (not all verses will be of equal significance).

Reference	praise*	teach	respond	encourage	other	unclear
			PURPOSES			
'music'						
Gen 31:27						
Jdg 5:3						
1 Sam 18: 6,7						
1 Chr 6: 31, 32						
1 Chr 15:16						
1 Chr 23:5						
1 Chr 25: 6,7						
2 Chr 5: 13; 7:6						
Neh 12:27						
Ps 27:6						
Ps 33:2						
Ps 57:7						
Ps 81:1-2						
Ps 87:7						
Ps 92:1-3						
Ps 95:1-2						
Ps 98:4-9						
Ps 144:9						
Isa 30: 32						

* Remember that to 'praise' God means to recall and proclaim his deeds and character

Reference	praise*	teach	respond	encourage	other	unclear
Amos 5:23						
Eph 5:19						
'sing'						
Ex 15:1						
Jdg 5:3						
2 Sam 22:48-50						
1 Chr 16:8-9						
1 Chr 16:23, 33						
Ps 7:17						
Ps 9:11						
Ps 13:6						
Ps 27:6						
Ps 33:1-3						
Ps 47:6						
Ps 51:14						
Ps 57:7						
Ps 61:8						
Ps 68:4						
Ps 71:22-23						
Ps 89:1						
Ps 95:1-2						
Ps 96:1-2						
Ps 98:1						
Ps 101:1						
Ps 105:2						
Ps 135: 3						
Ps 145:7						
Ps 147:1						
Ps 149:1,5						
Isa 12:5						
Isa 52:8-9						
Jer 20:13						
1 Cor 14:15						
Eph 5:19-20						
Col 3:16						
Jas 5:13						
Rev 5:13						
Rev 15:2-3						

Reference	praise*	teach	respond	encourage	other	unclear
'song'						
Deut 31:19-22						
Ps 18: title						
Ps 28:7						
Ps 40:3						
Ps 42:8						
Ps 45: title						
Ps 69:30						
Ps 92: title						
Ps 144:9						
Isa 42:10						
Rev 5:9						

Try to summarize in a couple of sentences what you have found the Bible says about music and singing.

Think it Through

1. How does this information affect:

   a. Our understanding of what music should be used for in church.

   b. The sort of music we choose to use in church.

2. In your own church, how do you use music at the moment? Is this right or wrong? In what areas do you need to make changes?

Being a Christian and a musician 5

by Greg Clarke & Rosalie Milne

Music in the world and the church

Think it through

1. Think of all the places that you hear music these days. For each situation, write down the type of music you expect to hear and the purpose for which the music is being used:

Situation	Type of Music	Purpose
e.g. supermarket	easy listening	making customers feel happy and relaxed
Coke ad on TV	rock or pop	to excite you, to make you feel young & fun, to make you want Coke

Situation	Type of Music	Purpose

2. What major similarities and differences stand out between the Bible's and the world's use of music?

3. Discuss the importance of these elements of music and performance:
   a. in the world
   b. in the church

   • style of music
   a.

   b.

   • a song's message
   a.

b.
- a musician's image and attitude
    a.

    b.

- musical excellence
    a.

    b.

- evoking of emotions
    a.

    b.

- audience's response
    a.

    b.

- having new songs
    a.

    b.

Dealing with problems

1. What particular problems face musicians in their task of serving the church?

2. On the following page is a list of approaches to common situations we face in church. Assess whether these statements are true or false (or, perhaps, half-true!) and carefully explain the reasoning behind your answers. (It may help to refer to other parts of this handbook).

- We should allow the tastes of the congregation to determine which songs we sing.

- A song with a great tune and average lyrics will be better than one with an average tune and great lyrics.

- If a song isn't working, you should stop in the middle of it and start again or choose a new one.

- It's best to let your minister choose the songs.

- Anyone who wants to serve the church by playing an instrument should be allowed to do so.

- We should encourage people to experience the emotional impact of what they are singing.

- When the singing is bad, the whole service is bound to have a bad feel about it.

- The ministry of music in church is as important as any other ministry.

3. For each of the following situations, discuss the *problems* and *principles* involved in coming to a solution which honours God and serves the people involved.

a. Your organist has been playing at the morning communion service for almost fifteen years. She is well-known and loved by the congregation, which is a mixture of young families and old women, but she is starting to lose her eyesight and her arthritis means that her playing is now very poor. Half the congregation enjoys the hymns she plays (she despises choruses), regardless of how they sound, but the other half would like some fresh music and fresh musicians.

- Should the organist be replaced?
- Should more modern music be introduced?

b. Your best pianist is totally unco-operative, rarely comes to rehearsals (but still plays brilliantly) and always wants to play solo sections. Most of the congregation love his playing, but the other musicians feel harassed and angry. He claims that they are simply jealous of his talent and the attention he gets.

- What should be done about the pianist?

- What should be done about the other musicians?

c. The music at your church has been appalling for some time. You only have a handful of committed but mediocre musicians in your small congregation and very little money to spend on equipment. The songleader has become discouraged and no longer wants to continue, saying, "It's embarrassing to lead such poor quality music". Someone has suggested that you contact musicians from other churches, or pay non-Christian musos to play.

- Should either suggestion be taken up?

d. The favourite songs of the moment happen to be slightly out of kilter with your church's teaching. People often request that they be sung and talk about the fact that other churches sing them and your church is a bit behind the times. Your minister doesn't want to sing them, but he has no appreciation of what makes a good song.

- How will you decide what songs to play?

e. You have been asked to organise music for a large weekend conference for teenagers. A number of musicians whom you don't know have called you, asking to play. You have also been informed that one of your congregation members is very upset that she wasn't chosen to play. One of the Bible teachers for the weekend informs you beforehand that one of the singers you have chosen is very unreliable and 'showy'. It becomes obvious that being a muso at the conference carries a high prestige value! In fact, you are beginning to wonder about your own motives in leading the music.

- How will you deal with each of these potential problems?

Summary of both studies

1. What have you learnt about the Bible's teaching on music?

2. What important principles for playing music in church have you learnt?

3. What personal changes do you need to make to be a better servant of God's people?

4. PRAY about these things, giving thanks for your opportunity to serve God's people.

Part III :

Practicalities

A series of short chapters
giving practical advice on
everything from songleading
to driving the PA.

The music director

6

by Sally Trethewey

What are the essential qualities for a Christian church music director? A sound knowledge of music theory? An ability to work with people? A good ear and a feel for what works musically? A good sense of rhythm?

All these are no doubt important, but the primary quality for a music director, as for anyone involved in any sort of Christian service or leadership, is personal godliness through relationship with Jesus Christ. Christian leadership is about service, and the humble use of gifts for the benefit of others. It is very important that the musical co-ordinator or director have a keen grasp of this point, and be someone who is distinguished not only by musical skill but by personal holiness; a person of prayer, and a regular and obedient reader of God's Word; a person who meets regularly with other Christians for mutual encouragement and who is concerned for the salvation of outsiders.

How can such personal godliness translate into practical action for a church music director or leader?

The godly music director is concerned that people are built up in their knowledge of God through the music at Christian meetings. At the same time, he or she will understand that the music ministry is subservient to the teaching ministry. To this end, his or her responsibility will be to reinforce this principle in dealings with church members and to develop rapport and sensitive communication with the church leader(s) to facilitate this principle.

Music and musicians have the potential to be distractions from the Word of God, and so the music director should foster a team (not individual) approach to playing congregational music, with all musicians working together to facilitate the group singing. He or she will be committed to encouraging all musicians to growth in their personal godliness and team spirit, punctuality and reliability, regular practice and an attitude of service.

In a large church, the music director would be wise to delegate responsibilities for co-ordinating each congregation's music programme to mature Christians, whose music ministry he or she regularly monitors and encourages. He or she should oversee the choice of music team members who are committed to Jesus, are regular church attendants and have adequate technical skills.

Another part of the music director's function should be to research, listen to and evaluate new, biblically reliable music for use in church. He or she should spend prayerful and regular time studying passages of Scripture to find the most suitable songs and/or hymns to fit the sermon and service theme(s).

It is important for the music director to remain adaptable and open minded, and to use wise counsel in discerning the effectiveness of the music ministry. He or she should evaluate and encourage the use of any appropriate new music to keep the material vital, relevant and varied. They should also observe (perhaps at other churches or conferences) how other Christian groups conduct their music ministry and select proven, successful methods of leading and teaching songs to the Christian community.

As noted above, the relationship between the church leadership and the music director is critically important for building the effectiveness and flexibility of a church's music program.

First, the music director should know the plans and intentions of the church leadership in order to understand how music fits into the overall congregational service and/or ministry structure. A godly leader is primarily concerned with Scriptural preaching, and secondly, how the whole meeting will operate, with music playing an integral (but not indispensable) role.

The music director should try to meet regularly with the church leaders to discuss and design the weekly or monthly music program, introduce them to new material and check the theology of selected songs. Such regular communication before, and feedback after, the church meeting should help establish and build a trusting relationship between the leader and music director. If the church leaders are assured of the music director's right attitude and commitment to a scripturally sound, high quality music ministry, they will be more likely to allow greater freedom for the development and implementation of a varied programme.

Everyone (including church leaders) has personal musical preferences which reflect personal taste, background and exposure to different styles of music. These preferences may be extensive or limited. A church leader with limited tastes has the potential to evoke frustration and irritation in a more expansive-thinking and experienced music leader. Such a situation should be handled with sensitivity and patience. The conscious (not manipulative) building of respect for the leader's wisdom and experience in their own areas of knowledge and expertise can help offset a critical mindset concerning their musical limitations.

It may be a strategic move to negotiate and, at times, acquiesce, to the leader's personal preferences for particular songs or hymns, rather than always disputing their validity. Introduce church leaders to new material regularly. Use logical explanations of why certain songs are appropriate in a particular context. Confer with them when the musical tastes of church members threaten to cause divisiveness in a meeting, and bring to their attention the fact that all Christians should understand the place of music in church, to counteract this tendency.

In summary, then, the most important qualities of a music director are personal godliness, a commitment to support the teaching ministry and to serve God and others with the musical leadership role that has been assigned them. While there are many ways these principles are worked out in practice, without these qualities, the music director will ultimately fail in the task, which is simply to be part of the one great Cause, along with all the other members of the congregation—to build God's church.

Choosing songs 7

by Rob Smith

'Song' is a general term used to describe quite a wide range of musical and lyrical forms, including hymns, choruses, liturgical music and even chants. In giving thought to the kinds of songs Christians sing when we come together, it is valuable to have some understanding of the different types of songs that exist and what makes them different from each other.

The following three categories ought to provide a helpful starting point for understanding most of the music we sing in our churches, although it must be admitted that many songs will contain a mixture of these elements.

Types of songs

1. Songs of Direct Address

Many songs are directly addressed, in one way or another, to God. For instance, a song that starts 'I love you, Lord' is addressing God in his sovereignty; a song that begins 'Father, I thank you' is directed to God by his child or children. Songs of direct address are extremely useful as vehicles for expressing wonder, thanks and love—particularly if the words are good.

Songs of this kind can also take the form of a joint petition or even confession of sin (e.g. 'Create in me a clean heart', which is based on Psalm 51).

This type of song generally contains a strong emotional component—it will appeal to people's emotions and draw a response. This can be very helpful in assisting people to respond to the Word of God in an appropriate and biblical way after hearing a Scripture reading or a sermon. However, this emotional component also has the potential to be unhelpful in that it can suggest that a certain type of emotional response ought to be present in those who are singing. This in turn can lead to a false and sometimes crushing sense of guilt in the person who doesn't *feel* what they think they ought to feel. Our emotional states vary for all sorts of reasons. Therefore, songs which demand of us a response that is, perhaps, unrealistic (because of the level of emotion required) or unbiblical (such as suggesting the desire to touch Jesus) should be avoided.

To my mind, the most valuable examples of this type of song are those which stay very close to the Scriptures, such as the *Fisherfolk* song 'Great and Wonderful', which is taken from Revelation 15:3-5.

2. Songs of confession

These songs are generally more objective in nature, seeking to tell out the great things that God has done. For this reason, they are usually more theological and credal and may be taken directly from Scripture. Whatever the case, they are a kind of proclamation in song and for this reason they are enormously valuable in building understanding and faith, and in making the gospel known.

In songs of confession we are not so much singing to God, but before him and to others, that is, to each other and to the world. However, we would be foolish to think that this makes it a lesser act of praise. In fact, the form that praise most commonly takes 'n the Scriptures is precisely that of 'recounting the mighty deeds of God' (see Ex 15: 1-18; Pss 103, 104, 106, 111, 147, et al.).

Some examples of the kind of song I am talking about are 'The Servant King' by Graham Kendrick, 'Jesus is Lord' in *Scripture in Song II* and many of the great old hymns, such as 'And Can It Be?', 'Before the Throne of God Above' and 'Amazing Grace'. There is a great need for more contemporary songs to be written in this vein—there is a challenge to all modern Christian songwriters!

In my opinion, the majority of the songs we sing should be of this type, for the reasons I have given. Moreover, songs of this kind also have a teaching function—a good reason for their theology being sound and helpfully expressed—and can, therefore, be used to support and reinforce the preached

Word. The fact is that people tend to remember what they sing. If they are singing the great truths of God's Word, this can only benefit them.

3. Songs of exhortation

These songs seek to exhort, challenge, encourage and inspire us to actions, such as telling out the gospel, loving one another, persevering in prayer and pursuing holiness. With this type of song we are again singing to each other with the specific aim of urging each other to obedience. This, of course, greatly pleases God and is likewise part of our praising him. We could also do with more songs of this kind.

Again, many of the Psalms fall into the category of exhortations to be 'up and doing', particularly in the matter of declaring God's praise among the nations, or as we like to call it, 'evangelism' (e.g. Pss 66, 95, 96,98,100,105, 107, 136, 148, et al.).

How to select songs

A number of factors should be kept in mind when choosing songs, be it for a church service, a youth night or a small home group. Of course, there are a great many factors to consider, such as the size of your meeting and the available musicians, but the questions below are of primary importance.

1. Are you using an integrated theme?

It is sometimes helpful to choose songs that follow a particular line of thought or have a common focus (e.g. the cross of Jesus). This would make sense in a service where the aim is to integrate the music with the Bible teaching. However, there is no reason why a service should not have more than one significant theme. The main questions to consider are 'Why are we singing these particular songs?' and 'In what order would it be most helpful to sing them?'.

2. Does the song reflect the truth of God's Word?

This may seem a fairly obvious thing to say, but an enormous number of Christian songs are full of nonsense. I used to be more lenient toward songs with lousy theology but a catchy tune, but I have come to see some of the destructive long-term effects that these kinds of songs produce. They need to be weeded out! If the case in point is a hymn with three good verses and one bad one, then leave the bad one out and sing the rest.

Of course, it is possible to over-react and go on a kind of 'witch hunt' and this needs to be avoided. Perhaps a simple test is to ask people what they think a particular song means. Some songs simply need to be explained before they can be helpfully sung.

3. Have you achieved the best balance?

Keeping in mind the different types of songs that we identified earlier, work at getting a balance (or a deliberate imbalance, as I suggested, with more confessional and less emotionally-oriented songs).

However, 'balance' also has to do with other factors such as the tempo, key and mood of the songs. For instance, if all the songs are the same speed, or if they are all pitched too high, the congregation may get bored and/or exhausted. These practical problems must be kept in mind.

Are we making use of our resources?

Christian congregations today are blessed with an enormous range of resources to draw upon. New music is being made available all the time (unfortunately, not all of it good) and many congregations are writing their own material. However, some of the most valuable resources we have are the hymns that have been bequeathed to us by past generations. These ought to be used if at all possible, since many of them are full of rich theology. Where the language is old-fashioned, this can often be changed (if so desired). Moreover, alternative tunes can be used and even new tunes written to many of the old hymns. The tune can, in many ways, make or break a hymn.

Finding new resources that are good takes time and effort. Ask people from other churches about what they are using. Take a trip to your local Christian bookstore and obtain music catalogues where they are available. Follow up songs that are used at conventions. There are plenty of avenues to explore in search of good material.

Are we committing this ministry to God?

Finally, but perhaps most importantly, pray about choosing songs for an occasion. Ask God for wisdom and help, in order that the songs you choose may bring blessing to those who sing them and serve to reinforce the ministry of the Word of God.

Riding the tiger 8

Dealing with music and emotions

by Tony Payne

Music hath charms, it is said, to calm the savage beast. But its charms are not always calming. As Rob Smith and others have already mentioned, music is an inherently emotional medium, and a powerful one at that. It has power to stir us and to quieten us, to fill us with joy or melancholy. Throughout the world, music is recognized as a means not just of stirring emotions, but of altering consciousness—for example, in the repetitive trance-inducing chanting of some Eastern and voodoo-style religions.

The Bible freely acknowledges the connection between emotion and song, and encourages the expression of emotion in song, especially joy. "Is any one of you in trouble? He should pray. Is anyone happy? Let him sing songs of praise" (James 5:13).

Emotions are part of the way God has made us, and music can function as a helpful way of expressing these emotions corporately as we gather together. If we are rejoicing at the salvation God has won for us, what better way to give vent to that joy than to raise our voices together in a great shout of jubilation?

However, emotions are powerful things, and music can be a powerful tool not only to express them, but also to manipulate them. In working out how to use music for the good of God's people, we need to be aware of the dangers as well as the possibilities.

Dangers

Let us deal with the negatives first. Perhaps the most common mistake is to confuse the 'feeling' of being close to God with the reality of being in relationship with him. Because music can stir us and move us so powerfully at times, it is tempting to identify this emotional response with a spiritual response, as if the quality of our music-induced feeling equalled the quality of our response to God.

This is dangerous ground. The Scriptures urge us to respond to God in repentance and faith—that is, in daily and continually turning from sin, and trusting in God as the one who alone can save us through Jesus Christ. This may be accompanied by strong emotions, or it may not be. The emotions vary from personality to personality, and from situation to situation. We must be careful of using the intensity of our feeling (and music can often boost this intensity) as a kind of spiritual barometer.

In a fascinating passage in 2 Corinthians 7, Paul talks of how he grieved the Corinthians with his letter to them. He hurt them, and they were in anguish. He goes on to say:

> Yet now I am happy, not because you were made sorry, but because your sorrow led you to repentance. For you became sorrowful as God intended and so were not harmed in any way by us. Godly sorrow brings repentance that leads to salvation and leaves no regret, but worldly sorrow brings death.
> 2 Corinthians 7:9-10

Note the implications of this. It is not the sorrow itself which is the key thing, for there can be godly sorrow that leads one to repent, or worldly sorrow that issues only in despair and death. The emotion may not tell us anything, one way or the other. It is the **repentance** that matters. Much the same can be said about music: it is not the emotion which the music might engender that signifies true repentance and faith, but a changed heart/mind and behaviour.

This is something which, as church musicians, we need to hear. There is a great temptation to use music to make people **feel** like they are close to God. This is not difficult to do. We have all heard stories, no doubt, about churches which use long, repetitive singing sessions to whip their congregations into an emotional frenzy (I could tell you one or two from my own early Christian days). We may not be out on that extreme, but the impact of this style of church singing has been widespread over the past 30-40 years. You can see its influence when church services start with a 'worship' time which consists largely of singing, and which seeks to elicit an emotional response from the congregation (by the choice of songs, their repetition, the instrumentation, the gestures and postures which accompany the singing, and so on.)

While we shouldn't feel inhibited about expressing our emotions in song, we also need to be careful about building an atmosphere that fosters false spirituality. I remember, as a young Christian, feeling the pressure to close my eyes and half raise my hands, and look as 'spiritual' as everyone else. Perhaps I was the only one there struggling with the insincerity of my devotional posturing, but given the universality of sin, I suppose I wasn't.

We need to be clear in our own minds as to the purpose of singing in church (see the articles in Part I) and be careful to communicate this to the congregation, both in the songs we sing and how we sing them.

Be thoughtful about feelings

Let me now suggest that while emotions can be dangerous and must be treated with care (especially by musicians), they are also inescapable. All music moves us emotionally—that is the nature of the medium. It may leave us feeling sad, happy, joyful, exuberant, determined, courageous or just bored, but it will have an effect. The effect will vary in intensity from person to person, but it will be there.

The key to handling the emotional side of music is not to deny it, nor to suppress it, but to use it for the encouragement of the church. This means being aware of the likely emotional consequences of a particular congregational song, and then using it appropriately in the meeting.

Some of this we do instinctively. We usually don't open our gatherings with slow, melancholy, lament-style numbers. We sense instinctively that this wouldn't be a good note on which to kick things off. But what would be a good note? This depends on your goals at that particular point of proceedings. You might want something strong and stirring to wake everyone up and signal that things are starting to happen (although strong, stirring hymns can fall decidedly flat if only half the congregation has arrived by starting time); or perhaps you might decide on a well-known, bright, breezy, enjoyable number to get everybody relaxed and ready to begin.

The point is that every song we use will have its effect on how people are feeling. We cannot avoid this, so we must harness that effect to godly ends. This is why it is so important for the person leading the meeting to work closely with the musicians. The music needs to fit into the structure of the gathering, not just in terms of content, but in terms of the emotions which it evokes and expresses. The music will tend to take the congregation 'up' or 'down' (to varying degrees, depending on the song) and we need to be aware of this and choose our music appropriately. Failure to do so can be disastrous.

I remember being the young and inexperienced song-leader at a Christian conference of about 300 people (mostly under 30). It was the evening session, and we'd already had a few songs, some prayer and a Bible reading, when I stood up and said, "Just before Pastor X comes to speak to us, let's sing again. We haven't quite got a thousand tongues here to sing God's praise, but let's give it our best." The band let fly (with its electric guitar, keyboard, trumpets, bass and drums), the overhead went up, and we launched into an electrifying rock version of "O for a thousand tongues". It was fantastic. By verse 6, the rafters were shaking, the whole group was all but dancing, and the electric guitarist had run out of volume on the amp. The song finished, and with difficulty everybody sat down. The room was alight. The emotional hype level was off the end of the scale. Whatever we were all ready for, one thing we weren't ready for was to sit quietly and attentively and listen to God's word being expounded. For the next 10 minutes, the MC for the evening did what he could to calm everyone down, in the end resorting to a long prayer. The song had been great, but the meeting was all but ruined by my thoughtless use of it at the wrong place in proceedings.

We need to think carefully about the emotional impact of the songs we choose and match them to their place in our meetings. For example, before prayer, the Bible reading or the sermon, if we are going to sing, we should choose songs that quieten the congregation and prepare them (in mood and content) for what is to follow. Similarly, after we pray in confession of our sins, that is surely the time for a song of joy as we celebrate the forgiveness God has granted us in Christ. All this requires a certain sensitivity—to what is happening at each point in the meeting, and to the likely effect of the music—plus a willingness to experiment and to learn from your mistakes.

To illustrate what I'm talking about, here's an outline of a fictitious evening evangelistic church meeting with an explanation of how the singing might fit into the flow of the meeting.

The goal for the meeting is to make visitors feel welcome and comfortable, and ready to hear the gospel explained. The congregation is of mixed ages, with the majority being 25-30 years old. The meeting is designed to be fairly short (not much more than an hour) and, because it is specifically evangelistic, there is not much corporate prayer.

The band consists of a piano, bass, rhythm guitar, flute, clarinet and trumpet. It was decided not to use the pipe organ so as to make the evening feel less formal and 'churchy'.

1. Song-leader opens the meeting and introduces first song: Sing a new song to the Lord (seated)

   This is a positive, bright, enjoyable, upbeat song which tends to put a spring in your step. As people are coming in and taking their seats—and they no doubt still will be at this point—this sort of song helps to create a relaxed and positive sort of atmosphere. It is not too formal or serious, yet it is not vacuous either. This is sung with everyone seated so that people can easily find their places.

2. The MC offers a more extended welcome, explains the format of the meeting, something of what is to come and prays briefly.

3. Song: The victory song (standing)

   This, again, is uptempo, feel-good kind of music, but not too long. It might be a bit of an oldy for many of the congregation, but not for the visitors. It has an air of celebration to it, and gives the meeting a lively impetus. It is not the sort of music visitors would be expecting to sing in church.

   Song-leader teaches new song: Amazing Love (seated; learn first verse and chorus)

   This is a song the congregation does not know, so it puts the church members and their invited guests in the same boat. We are all learning something new together. This is the song we will sing later after the sermon, and so learning it now also anticipates some of the themes of the talk. Being a quieter, more serious number, it also quietens the meeting down in preparation for the interview that follows.

5. MC interviews congregation member about their conversion, the difference Christ makes to their life, etc. The MC prays, thanking God for what he has done in this person's life, and for his goodness to all of us.

6. Same congregation member then reads the Bible passage to be preached.

7. Song: Worthy the lamb (standing; done first in unison, then as two-part round; last time unaccompanied).

> This short round has several advantages: it is about Jesus' death (the theme of the gospel message); it is short and easy to pick up for the newcomer; and sung as a round it is quietening, even haunting, in its emotional effect. It is the kind of song that leaves the meeting in almost absolute silence, in which the speaker can step forward and begin his address.

8. Sermon

9. Concluding song: Amazing Love (standing)

> This is the song learnt earlier. It expresses something of the wonder and joy at the love of Christ in dying for us, and is thus appropriate as a response to the gospel message. It is somewhat majestic in feel, but without being too sombre. That it is contemporary in idiom and music is also helpful.

This sample outline is only for one meeting, and a specialized evangelistic one at that, but it illustrates the way we ought to be thinking about how singing fits into our gatherings.

Emotions are part of God's good creation. We can rejoice (there's an emotion) that God has made us this way, and that our relationship with God will be accompanied by, and expressed in, various emotions.

However, let us put emotions in their right place. Let us not suppress our feelings, as if it is inappropriate to feel strongly about God, and to express this. But let us also not confuse our feelings with the closeness to God that comes only through Jesus Christ. We are close to God because our true life is hidden with Christ in God (Col 3:1-3).

Leading and teaching songs

9

by Rosalie Milne

So, the team of musicians is chosen, the music has been selected in liaison with the minister and everyone is ready to rehearse...except the songleader. Pity.

There is far more to songleading than singing into a microphone and waving the arms in ever-increasing figures of eight.

What is it that makes a songleader 'good'?

It should be noted at this point that the following discussion arises not from an 'expert' in the field, but from someone who has had some experience in songleading (and more particularly, some painful experiences!) and who will always benefit from more experience.

As with any other position of leadership, it is important that the songleader take his or her responsibility seriously as a leader of musicians and the people in the congregation.

The role of songleader is not only a practical musical role, but carries with it the challenge of marrying the Scriptural understanding of our relationship with God with musical enhancement and enjoyment. While the choice of the songs will set the standard, the way in which the music is interpreted will determine the final outcome. A significant part of that final outcome lies in the attitude of the songleader and an understanding of service in a Christlike manner.

Philippians 2:1-11 cannot be quoted too often to the songleader who stands in a position which potentially can either draw great attention to himself, or give great honour to God and his purposes.

So who would be a songleader?

It is a rather good start if the songleader is musical and can confidently lead the melody. It is also of great benefit if the songleader has had the experience of being in the position of musician or singer since that will provide him or her with the necessary empathy for those who are being led and directed.

The need for preparation cannot be overemphasized. The songleader should allow enough time to rehearse the music thoroughly. This will necessarily take more time than just playing the piece through; time is required both for arranging the music with the balance of instruments, style and mood, and particularly for teaching a new song to both the musicians and the congregation. The songleader should therefore be familiar with the music before introducing it to the musicians.

Once the songleader has determined the length of time necessary for rehearsal, he or she should set practice times, inform the musicians and expect attendance. For the sake of the rest of the musicians, consistent late attendance of a musician should be followed up by the songleader.

In determining the **physical arrangement** of the musicians, it is very helpful that the musicians have eye-contact with the songleader and not be reliant on the songleader's hand movements alone. This is particularly important for the keyboard player, who plays a strong role in leading the musicians.

The position and layout of the musicians should not be too distinct from the congregation (unwittingly giving the musicians the appearance of superiority) and should not distract the congregation, either during singing or at other times in the meeting.

In **interpreting and enhancing the music of a song**, the style chosen must be sympathetic to the message of the lyrics and appropriate to its place in the program (e.g. a contemplative song after a sermon or talk will not be effective if sung at double pace).

The choice of instruments and arrangement will also assist in bringing a song to its full potential. High sounds, providing melodic lead and 'brilliance' will be achieved by using the flute, trumpet, voice and piano.

Medium sounds, giving richness and 'body', will be achieved using the organ, clarinet and strings. Low sounds, giving rhythm and 'feel', will be achieved using drums, guitars and bass.

Harmonies, rounds, responsive singing, unaccompanied verses and musical interludes are some of the ways that the music can be varied and strengthened in effectiveness. Skilled and accommodating musicians can be a great asset to the songleader in offering suggestions and alternative arrangements.

The songleader can assist the congregation by checking the 'singability' of the song. A song may be simplified, the key changed or the rhythm accentuated to help the congregation when bewilderment is written all over their faces. If this bewilderment can be anticipated *before* the event, all the better!

During the rehearsal time, it is a good idea to play and sing through the song as though it is the 'real thing', using the hand movements and directions which will later be used.

Musical introductions should be clear and well practised, as should conclusions, repeats and variations. Difficult phrases should be repeated and it is always a good idea to check that everyone is confident before moving on.

Once the song is well played, interesting variations can be discussed and agreed upon and the songleader and musicians should make notes to remind themselves of special pointers.

Verbal introductions to songs should be carefully thought through so that they are not ineffectual or a replacement for the sermon. It does little to suggest that people 'really think about this song', but it may be effective to draw the congregation's attention to a line or two of the lyrics.

Where the songleader is confident of his or her timing, a conducted, timed introduction of one or two bars will set the pace for the group. However, if a song is racing away or becoming a dirge, or the group or songleader 'loses it', don't be afraid to begin again or stop.

Every songleader has, at one time or another, been through the painful experience of hearing the music come tumbling down around his or her ears. At that excruciating time, use your sense of humour and move on. People *do* understand, and ongoing apologies will only make the situation worse, as together everyone crawls under their chairs!

Conducting a group of people may or may not be appropriate, depending on the size of the group and the particular situation. There is no 'correct' school of conducting and each individual songleader needs to feel comfortable and relaxed with his or her own style. The personality of the individual will affect much of what he or she does and we can be thankful for those God-given differences.

In the early days of conducting, it is sometimes helpful to conduct in front of a mirror to gain feedback on the size of hand movements used and general presentation. If hand movements are to be used, they should be helpful and clear, indicating information such as timing (e.g. 3/4 time), tempo, volume and feel of the song.

Examples of possible hand movements are as follows:

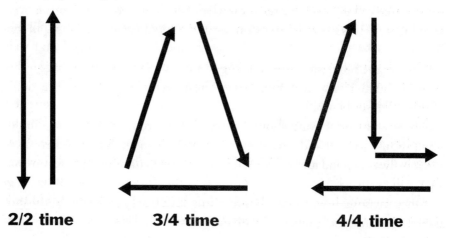

2/2 time   **3/4 time**   **4/4 time**

The speed of a song can be indicated by the pace at which the song is conducted. The conclusion of a song could be slowed down by raising both hands rather than just one, to gain the attention of the congregation, and 'hand-stepping' the last line or two of the song.

Large, full hand and arm movements will indicate increased volume, and small movements will indicate decreased volume. It is important, therefore, for songleaders not to use all their energy in the first verse!

The 'feel' of the song may be indicated with hand and body movements and facial expressions. A gentle song could be conducted using smooth 'figure of eight' hand movements, while 'military-like' music could be conducted using strong and definite hand and arm movements as illustrated above.

Some important points to remember in leading, whether by conducting or leading from the guitar or keyboard, are to be confident, to communicate clearly with words and hand movements, to establish regular eye contact with the congregation and musicians and to try to be as relaxed as possible (though this is sometimes easier said than done!).

While songleaders are encouraged to take their role seriously, they don't always need to be serious. The relaxed and comfortable songleader will generally produce the same attitude in the congregation.

Once a songleader is confident with leading the musicians and the congregation, the next step is to **learn how to teach a song to a congregation**. Directions for teaching these songs need to be well thought through by the songleader. The process of learning a new song should be enjoyable and not overwhelming or dazzling for the congregation.

A new song should be sung and played through to demonstrate at least one example of a verse or chorus and how they relate together.

The song should then be broken down into the logical or natural phrases or parts to be taught. These phrases should be pre-arranged and well rehearsed with the musicians, providing clear introductions, stops and repeats.

Difficult phrases or word phrasings should be taught and repeated separately and then incorporated into the whole verse or chorus. Some complicated parts may need to be simplified for congregational use. New songs will generally need to be taught more slowly than the speed at which they will eventually be sung, depending on the difficulty of the song.

Clear stepped hand movements will help to teach and then reinforce a new song to a congregation. These steps should be relative to the distance between the notes of the song e.g. when moving from a middle C to an octave above, a large step will be used in contrast to moving from C to the next note of D. The use of stepped hand movements should continue until the congregation is singing very confidently.

It is important that the melody line be strongly taught and emphasised while the people are learning the song. The melody may be played clearly using such instruments as the keyboard, flute, trumpet, violin or voice.

It is only when the people are confident with the song that vocal parts or descants should be introduced (preferably with an additional singer), or instrumental improvisation and harmony used.

Once a song is learned, it should be repeated, at least in the following week or session, to reinforce it. It should also be noted that on a weekend conference, the saturation point for learning new material will probably be reached by the congregation before the musicians and songleader.

The many facets of song leading and song teaching will be refined through practice, practice and more practice. Improvements also come from sifting through the many comments and suggestions offered by reliable witnesses (and some unreliable witnesses) and attempting to make necessary changes.

So, the team of musicians is chosen, the music has been selected in liaison with the minister or leader and everyone is ready to rehearse... yes, even the songleader.

Songleading from the guitar 10

by Sally Trethewey

It is a very common sight in churches to see the songleader also playing the guitar. There are good musical reasons for this: singing and guitar playing are eminently compatible activities, if the success of rock music is any measure. The challenge to the guitar-playing songleader is to understand how to do both tasks well.

Singing and playing an instrument like guitar or keyboard always requires more concentration and effort than doing either activity on its own. More initial practice is required to become proficient at coordinating playing and singing, as is ongoing, regular preparation and rehearsal. Every musician has difficulty playing and singing certain pieces, often because the vocal and instrument rhythms are very different and difficult to co-ordinate.

Nevertheless, there are advantages for the church which has a competent guitarist/songleader. One obvious one is his or her mobility with the instrument, having the ability to play anywhere from youth group halls to home Bible study groups, houseparties to camp fires at a beach mission. Another advantage is that they are good musical accompaniment alone or with other instruments.

Functionally, the guitar is a rhythmic and harmonic instrument which is quite easy to learn to a reasonable level of competence. When played with versatility, the guitar can facilitate the singing of a wide variety of musical styles including rock, country, jazz, blues, pop, folk and ballads. The use of a guitar is ideal for informal, small gatherings. It is an ideal background for hearing song words and can help make Christian community singing appropriately personal and emotionally responsive to God's Word.

Guitar playing usually provides the rhythm, feel and pitch of a song, supporting the voice, which holds the melody. Therefore, the songleader needs to know the tune well—the task of playing *and* reading the words and chords is enough to cope with! In fact, if the songleader/guitarist is going to play smoothly, sing confidently and maintain regular eye contact with the congregation and lead them, *it is virtually essential to know the words and music by heart.* Practicing chord changes, simplifying difficult chords or using open chords, transposing songs into easier keys (and/or using a capo) are all ways which can help co-ordinate a song more effectively and efficiently. If you can't manage to learn it all by heart, writing out the chords in pencil above *all* the words in the music book can help you to get by.

Different songs lend themselves to different rhythms and methods of guitar playing. For example, ballads are often played softly using a picking style; songs with a 'country' or 'blues' feel usually require the use of a syncopated/rhythmic strumming style (using a plectrum). Knowing how to play a variety of rhythmic styles, and which styles work best with which songs, takes time and practice. Listening to recordings of good guitar playing and singing, or watching competent guitarists can accelerate the learning process. In the meantime, while improving, a budding singer/guitarist should try to organise song arrangements to suit his or her playing ability, only using a rhythm he or she can competently sing with. Many songs are very adaptable to different rhythms.

Unfortunately, not all aspiring guitarist/singers have the ability or competence for songleading using the guitar. There are a number of unhelpful factors which can detract from encouraging people to sing. Some examples include: poor guitar tuning; overplaying and/or 'performance' playing; ambivalent singing instructions; and wrong or hesitant chord changes. If people are unsure about their competence in any of these areas, it may be best to concentrate on getting either the playing or singing right and hand the other task to someone else.

On the other hand, the best guitarists and the best singers may not always make the best songleader/guitarists. People with reasonable aptitude, commitment to service and practice, and willingness to learn, can make singing with a guitar more enjoyable and edifying for the group than an individual who allows the focus to rest on his or her own abilities.

Guitarist/singers have logistical and equipment needs when they songlead:

- A sturdy music stand, personal 'page turner' and microphone boom stand (if playing in large venues) are necessary to give the instrument freedom of movement and allow the leader to get close enough to read the music and sing from the microphone.

- Other usual prerequisites include a guitar strap (for standing); an electronic tuner (for noisy rooms when time is short); a capo to change the key (allowing the continued use of easier, open chords); thumb picks, plectrums and perhaps finger picks; a guitar stand if playing intermittently throughout the meeting.

- Right-handed guitarists should always stand on the left side of a group of musicians or towards the right side of the 'stage' when they play alone. In the first instance, a moving guitar neck is less likely to hit other players. In the second, the guitar neck can swing backwards, allowing the player to see more of the congregation and to control the songleading with his or her body movement.

- When standing to play, the guitar strap should be adjusted so the guitar is not positioned too high on the body (restricts movement) nor too low (inhibits eye contact with the group and can create hunching). The leader is more likely to sit and play for small, informal gatherings (e.g. sitting in a circle), while in larger groups he or she can stand to be more easily seen.

A major restriction for guitarist/songleaders is that they are not 'hands free' to conduct and step-teach songs. This places greater importance on their verbal skills and facial and bodily expressions to communicate instructions. A certain amount of copying occurs with any songleading. However, cues and clues, such as telling the congregation the length of the musical introduction, key changes and difficult intervals or tempo changes, can compensate for not using hands and arms. Nodding, smiling, eye contact and guitar movement can also control the singing and communicate instructions between verses and/or choruses.

An easy personal style from the songleader/guitarist communicates ease and comfort to the group, helping to build rapport with them. While it is tempting to hide behind the guitar, looking down at the neck continually, avoiding eye contact with the singers is a poor method of communication. Eye contact and smiling are important tools which should be used to help lead. Practice playing and singing in front of the mirror at home and get valued friends to give feedback about your presentation in order to improve your poise and presentation.

The guitar is a rhythmic instrument, so the songleader/guitarist should avoid a nervously stiff posture and rigid style, instead feeling free to move by tapping a foot in time with the rhythm. At the other extreme, however, excessive movement (i.e. 'Elvis mode') will shift the focus from group singing to the performance of the individual player. Moving freely should make the songleading sound more relaxed and natural.

In conclusion, then, a competent, confident and ministry-minded songleader/guitarist can make a valuable contribution to the music ministry of any church or Christian group. They have great mobility and flexibility and the potential for providing variety to musical styles, feels and rhythms. Like any Christian musician, however, they must be committed to serving others with their gift, and prayerful and diligent in working this out in practice.

Vocal and presentation techniques

11

by Dallas Watts

Singing is not merely a matter of opening one's mouth and letting agreeable sounds stream forth. When leading singing or presenting singing items at church, we must think not only of the song, but also of the many elements which contribute to an effective presentation. The most important of these elements are appearance and ability, and each element has its own, time-honoured piece of proverbial advice.

Appearance

1. Dress

As Christians, we should not be caught up with image, but it is important to dress appropriately so that members of the congregation do not lose focus on the meeting and waste time gasping at the latest fashion. Of course, being appropriate will mean different things with different people. Modesty, however, is a biblical requirement.

Proverb 1: "When in Rome, wear what the Romans wear".

2. Energy

Whether or not songleaders like to admit it, a congregation expects to be cajoled, entertained, woken up and *led*. A congregation wants to feel secure with its songleader, so don't come across as tentative. Most of all, don't be afraid of making mistakes. In the case of items, be yourself and present yourself in keeping with the song you are singing.

Proverb 2: "It is more blessed to give generously of yourself than to be anxious".

3. Movement

A singer should move very quickly to the rostrum or lectern so that time is not wasted. Move confidently and with the expectation that something really worthwhile is going to take place. Your stance should be comfortable and relaxed. Make sure you acknowledge the different areas of the group when singing or leading a song. This should be done using both facial expressions and physical movements. A degree of physical openness should be apparent so that you address different phrases of a song to a variety of areas across the congregation.

Through your facial expressions, make it clear to the group how you feel about what you and they are singing. Aim to use your position of leadership to unite the congregation as they sing. The difference between 100 individuals singing in 100 different showers, and the community singing in a church gathering, is directly related to the songleader's endeavours to help the group sing together. When songleading, encouragement covers a multitude of sins.

Proverb 3: "Include all the disciples".

Ability

1. Vocal ability

It is important for the songleader to have a voice which others find enjoyable. However, if there is 'no one else available' to do the job, do your best and concentrate on your rapport with the congregation. If there is no one in your church who possesses leadership skills and who can sing in tune, it might be wise to delete choruses and concentrate on hymns, or just keep the choruses very simple. Greater vocal ability is needed for items. Songleaders should look to develop the ability they have, in order to do their job better.

Proverb 4: "God gives gifts that are needed to build the body".

2. Conducting

The first beat in the bar is nearly always the most important. 'Lean' vocally on the first note to make it easier for the congregation to follow you. If you have no microphone, it is important to conduct with one hand. If the group is large, you should use both hands and follow either a circular or square motion. The important thing is to move your hand(s) up on the last beat of the bar so that the next beat (the first beat of the next bar) receives the down-beat movement.

If you don't like 'schoolteacher-style' conducting, lead the group with facial and head movements. However, most people should use hand conducting. You need a very strong voice (or a microphone) if you aren't conducting by hand.

Proverb 5: "The first and then the last notes are most important".

3. Vocal technique

Whether you are using a microphone or classical technique, it is important to focus tone to the front of the mouth. When using a microphone, you only need to use 'head voice', as the mike provides all the projection required. However, if you are using a classical method, you must lean away from the mike to avoid shrill feedback.

The breath is most important, as it enables you to shape the phrases of a song and to sustain an attractive vocal line. Whatever stage you are in with regard to vocal development, remember that variety is terribly important and that certain words need to be imbued with meaning and emotion, while others are not so important.

Use your diaphragm: whether using classical or microphone technique, it is important to rest or support the voice to reduce strain on the vocal chords. Singing technique, like the Christian life, is full of paradoxes.

Proverb 6: "Think down for the high notes and up for the low notes".

Presenting an item

12

by Nicky Chiswell

There's nothing worse than a list of do's and don't's thrust on you when you're trying to be creative and imaginative, is there? Think, then, of the following comments as a collection of ideas that may help your item presentation to be powerful, not pathetic!

An item presented during a Christian meeting can do several helpful things:

- It can help people relax and feel OK about being at a Christian meeting, especially if it's a new thing for them. A song that they just listen to will be more relaxing than group singing.
- It can create variety in a meeting and stop people from 'switching off'.
- It can create a bridge between different parts of the meeting. For example, it can punctuate Bible readings and the talk, or separate the talk from the end of the meeting.
- It can make people's hearts beat a little faster as it helps the truth to make an emotional impact. This particularly is the case when the song follows the talk.

Keeping the *purpose* of the item in mind as you choose what to sing really helps it to work. The items that are most helpful are ones that fit in with the themes and ideas raised in the rest of the meeting. Here are some other ideas that may help:

- *Go for it! Be creative.* Don't be shy about your item. Look far and wide for appropriate songs. If a song to suit the meeting doesn't spring to mind, write one! I'm sure that the best sources of inspiration for old and new songwriters are a deadline and a sermon topic or passage (about 70% of my songs are inspired this way). You end up with meaty songs which are fuelled by God's Word and not just individual experience. I'm convinced there are many people around who can write decent songs and are just waiting for the opportunity. If you really feel you can't, then think ahead to commission someone else.

- *Know yourself.* Here's the psychological bit. The best performers don't perform an act—they express themselves. If performing somehow makes us feel like we are better than other people, we need to figure out *why*. We need to know ourselves. As we try to reach into the hearts of others with truth about God and the world, they will be able to tell if we are for real. They also can tell if we're just doing it to feel good about ourselves! The simplest song from the heart—'three chords and the truth'—is powerful. Virtuosic self-glorification doesn't really work in a Christian meeting.

- *Reach the outsider.* If the Christian meeting is particularly designed to include the unbeliever then I tend to think about the following ideas as I choose the material.

  If the item is to come *before* the talk, I pick songs that ask questions, raise relevant themes and introduce relevant ideas. I try not to steal the preacher's thunder by giving all the answers. Something popular and well known and not necessarily Christian can be appropriate. For example, I often sing "Will you still love me tomorrow?" if God's love is the theme of a meeting. I briefly introduce it by highlighting the uncertainty of human love.

  If the item is to come *after* the talk, I pick a song that is 'full-on Christian'! It needs to point to Christ; it must fit in with and add emotional impact to points made in the talk. Liaise with the speaker and plan ahead in order to do this well. Write your own material if you need to. Don't introduce an item directly after a talk: it 'breaks the spell' that the talk has woven.

Finally, here are a few practical tips on how to present an item. First, know the song backwards, practise heaps so that you can relax and enjoy it. The listeners will enjoy it more, too. If you are nervous and tentative, your listeners will feel the same way and miss the point of the item. Confidence also enables you to maintain important eye contact.

If you are playing or singing in a group, communicate well with each other and be as 'tight' as possible. This enhances the impact of the song and removes the distractions which come with sloppy presentation.

One last point: expressing appropriate emotion in presentation is important. However, there comes a point where 'schmaltz' and soppiness take over. I try to avoid confirming people's suspicions that Christianity and Christian music is sentimental 'goop'. A contemporary and clear style can help. Words that are strong and avoid cliches are good. A few weeks ago, after I had presented an item in a church meeting, a lady said to me, "That was great...it wasn't the slightest bit 'itemy'". I laughed, and felt greatly complimented.

Working as a team

13

by Rosalie Milne

Where does the songleader begin in choosing a team of musicians? Once the team is chosen, how can it be built up into a united and effective group which will in turn build up and encourage God's people?

There are a number of characteristics or qualities which mark a potentially good team member in a Christian setting, the first being that the musician is a Christian.

This may sound like a painfully obvious statement. However, it is vital that the songleader's first concern is for the well-being of the musicians in his care—for their relationship with God and the influence they will have upon the people whom they are serving.

Anyone who has been involved with music will understand how much of a commitment it can be in terms of thought and energy. It is therefore important that if a musician does not understand the gospel, he or she be given as few distractions as possible in order to give them every opportunity to listen and understand what is being said in the meeting.

Similarly, the songleader should be aware of the needs of Christian musicians. If someone is struggling or confused and needs some 'time out', it is important to give that person the opportunity to think and pray about his or her relationship with God and gather resources. No music program is more important than the spiritual well-being of the musician and the congregation.

A second quality essential to the work of a musical team is the understanding that people are not in the group to perform and display their musical prowess, but to glorify God and to serve the needs of his people. That is, a person's godliness is more important than his or her gifts, and a gift does not always have to be used.

However, this doesn't mean that the sound system should be turned off and bags placed over the heads of the musicians to avoid any possible recognition. Nor does it mean that the music should be played poorly, without rehearsal or utilising the skills and sensitivities of the individual musicians. Rather, the aim must always be to serve God and others instead of self.

Thirdly, a good team musician will display cooperation and flexibility. A team musician will attempt to complement the strengths and weaknesses of the other team members, both musically and personally. He or she will also attempt to accommodate the individual suggestions of the other musicians, driven by their individual styles and tastes. However, it is the songleader who sometimes has the unenviable task of deciding which ideas should and should not be used. It is here that he or she needs to pray for wisdom and sensitivity!

Another aspect of teamwork is being attentive and responsive to the songleader. This is particularly important for the keyboard player, who will play a major part in introductions and endings and in determining the feel of a song. While there is a place for spontaneity, the time for making changes to the arrangement of a song is during the *rehearsal*, not when it is being sung by 100 people.

No matter how talented and skilled a musician is, it is very important that he or she also be reliable and trustworthy. A musician who is caring for the rest of the team will make an effort to be punctual to rehearsals and events and will complete the tasks for which he or she has volunteered or been asked to do (e.g. bringing their music to the rehearsal or phoning other musicians).

It is a poor excuse for a musician to claim that he is so skilled that he doesn't need to be present for the entire rehearsal. The more skilled a musician is, the more he has to serve the less skilled or less confident musicians.

There is an underlying assumption that a musician should be technically competent and willing to practise songs to the level of competence required for a particular setting or event. It is obvious that a long weekend conference with multiple singing sessions and new material will require more rehearsal and skill than a weekly church gathering with familiar songs.

Valued team musicians are those who treat their role seriously in the ministry of music and prayerfully consider their contribution (both musically and personally) to the needs of the rest of the team and the people they are leading in music.

The songleader needs to choose the group of musicians carefully, rather than being faced later with the difficult situation of asking a musician to step down from his or her role. This can be damaging and confusing for the musician and impair his or her relationship with the songleader.

While the songleader may look carefully at the qualities of the individual musician, it is also worthwhile to consider how the whole group will work together with individual personalities and likes and dislikes. Some combinations just seem to work more effectively than others.

Once the team of musicians is chosen, it is the responsibility of the songleader to draw the team together, care for the needs of the individual members, and encourage them to use all of their combined skills and efforts to serve God and his people whom they are leading in music.

It is very important that the team pray together about the music, their part in the meeting and the total programme. By regularly working as a team and praying together, the musicians and songleader will be reminded of their common intention. When rifts or difficulties arise—as they surely will—the group is reminded of the need to be in relationship with God and each other.

It is important to care for the practical needs of the musicians and not to wear them out in rehearsal or by the length of time in any roster period. For weekly meetings, playing for one month and then having one month off gives people breathing space and time to be an 'ordinary' member of the congregation.

Church musicians, while committed to their role, should not feel that they will continually be fulfilling this role for all time. There may be times when they will fulfil a completely different role in their church, according to the needs around them. Being a church musician is not a matter of ongoing status or obligation—it's a matter of serving the needs of the congregation at that point in time.

As church musicians or music leaders, we need to pray that we will be examples of servanthood to the rest of our team, just as they will be for us.

Music and children   14

by Stephanie Carmichael

C hildren in church. Noisy, active, fun-loving children in church. Every congregation has them at some time or other, whether for a regular fifteen minutes before Sunday School or on the occasional school-holiday Sunday.

Do children and church music mix? I'd like to suggest that they certainly do, and in the following few pages deal with some of the issues involved in combining music and children. I am writing primarily with this 'family church time' in mind, although many of the points are applicable to music in the Sunday School (or even Beach Mission) setting as well. I will conclude by discussing the topic of leading a singing session for children only, such as in a Sunday School.

Considering children in a church meeting

First, however, let us think about children in the church meeting. If children are present in part or all of your church meeting, it is worthwhile singing children's songs for a number of reasons:

* it will give them a sense of belonging as they see that church is not just designed for adults

- it will encourage them to participate in church rather than simply watching or playing
- children learn and remember songs much better than just words alone, so songs are a powerful tool for teaching them truths which will stay with them for many years (perhaps all their lives)
- the simplicity of children's songs can be a reminder to Christian adults and a learning tool for non-Christian adults of the fundamentals of the Christian faith

Many of the things that have already been said in earlier chapters of this book apply to children's music in church. For example, being a servant—yes, even to children! Sometimes it is easy to be a musical servant to adults where you can display your talents and are appreciated. But a music ministry with children does not provide much kudos, nor does the music give much musical fulfilment—it tends to be very basic. Serving children with our music can be a good test of our sincerity. Having said this, I might add that there is at least one reward with which we are blessed, and that is seeing the enjoyment in the children's faces.

When children are in a church service, we often only think of them by including a children's song and then forget their presence when choosing other songs and hymns. I'm not suggesting 15 minutes of children's songs; rather I'm encouraging the thoughtful selection of hymns and adult songs. Avoid long hymns, those with 'old English' lyrics and those with difficult phrases (which adults may struggle to understand, too), unless a clear explanation can be given.

There is benefit for children in hearing hymns, so try and choose hymns which will create a positive impression. One idea for a compromise between a children's song and an adult's song would be a hymn with a simple chorus which the children could sing.

Choosing songs
As with music for adults, much care should be taken with choosing songs for children. There is even greater need to be careful with the truthfulness and helpfulness of the lyrics. When we simplify things for children there is great scope for distorting the truth, and less ability on the part of the singer to discern things which are not quite right.
Here are some other principles to keep in mind:

1   Don't just be attracted to catchy tunes with fun actions—as I've already begun to indicate, lyrics are very important. Songs must use

vocabulary and concepts which the children can understand. The meaning must be clear, without unhelpful or ambiguous phrases.

2   At the same time, short catchy songs with fun actions *and* good words will be remembered better than good words with boring music and no actions!

3   If there are any difficult words or phrases, preface the singing with a short, simple explanation so that children know what they are singing.

4   Songs should be short. The shorter the song, the more quickly and easily it will be learnt (which is particularly important for younger children who haven't learnt to read yet—they will be singing from memory). It's valuable to aim to memorise songs so that the hands are free for doing actions rather than holding songbooks. Avoid songs with numerous verses, unless they are fairly repetitive (i.e. only changing a few key words in each verse).

5   With shorter songs, introduce some variety by singing the same song a few different ways: e.g. using clapping or actions, breaking into parts, loudly/softly, fast/slow etc.

6   Actions are valuable because they aid memory, are fun for the children, encourage participation, assist concentration and, if adults can be persuaded to join in, they create interaction between the children and adults (which increases the fun for the kids and loosens up the adults!).

7   If you are singing more than one song in a church service, then choose one which will particularly appeal to the younger children and one that will appeal to the older children, so that everyone feels included.

Leading a children's song

Again there are a few basic principles:

1   It may sound obvious, but it is easy to forget: be visible and audible (to every child).

2   Be as close as possible to the children so that they feel included (for instance, try to avoid rows of empty pews between them and you).

3   Be enthusiastic and use exaggerated facial expressions. Show that you are enjoying it too! In fact, you will find that your enjoyment is contagious—if you convey that you are having fun then the children will want to join in the fun.

4   In everything you say to direct the children, use short, simple

Continued on page 100

Writing songs

If you can't find a suitable song then you may be able to write one. Before you decide you would never be able to, remember that:

- the tune need only be very basic
- familiar tunes can be used and you need only think of the words
- for young children, the simpler the song the better
- the words don't have to rhyme
- you don't need accompaniment in order to sing (more on this later)
- if you do have a pianist/guitarist, they can work out the appropriate chords

Example for Pre-School children (2-4 years)

If you want to teach or reinforce a particular message—don't forget to make sure that the message is biblical—writing a song can be a valuable tool. It is often difficult to find suitably simple songs for Preschoolers.

Let's say that the message you want the children to learn is that God loves them and that this is a cause for happiness. Here's how we could write a song to reinforce that message.

Message : God loves them. This is a cause for happiness.
Words : God loves me. God loves me.
 I can be happy for God loves me.
Tune : Think of a simple tune. I have just used three notes.

God loves me. God loves me. I can be happy for God loves me.

It is very simple, yet that is just what very young children need — something easy to learn, repetitive, and able to be easily extended with other verses (e.g. God made me, God knows me).

An alternative idea for a tune would be to put the words to a familiar tune (note: by this I don't necessarily mean a tune which the children know—so long as you know the tune well).

Example for children aged 5-7 years

Songs which are based on a Bible verse can be written for this age group and are an ideal way of reinforcing a message. At the time of writing the following song, our Sunday School was studying David, and in particular, 2 Samuel 7.

Bible verse: "How great you are, O Sovereign LORD! There is no-one like
you, and there is no God but you, as we have heard with our own ears."
(2 Sam 7:22).

How great you are O Lord. There is no one like you. How

great you are O Lord. There is no God but you.

Ideas for singing: This song lends itself well to percussion accompaniment or
clapping. For a variation, children could try alternately clapping once
on their knees and once with their hands—it all adds to their interest
and enjoyment.

Example for children aged 8-11 years

Make use of popular forms of music. Primary children are beginning to show
an interest in popular music and it is helpful if they see that the music at church
or Sunday School is modern. Most Primary children would find hymns and
dated songs boring (this isn't to say that you shouldn't use them occasionally).

Songs are a little more difficult to write for Primary children as they need
more depth than a simple Preschool or Infants' song. A good place to start is the
Bible. You may find a verse or passage which is relevant to what is being studied
and which could form the basis of a song.

Try to use a currently popular form of music (e.g. rap) and encourage the
children to participate creatively, even in the writing of the songs.

To illustrate how children can be involved in writing songs, here's an
example of a song written by a 9-year-old. (Thanks, Rachel Manchester, for
your song.)

Words: Thank you, Father, for all good things you give
                  Thank you, Father, for all I have to live
                  I want to share with others
                  I want everyone to see
                  That I thank you, Father, for always loving me.

Tune: "Ten Green Bottles"

explanations. Don't give long introductions—you'll lose them before you've even started.

5   Make it clear when the children are to begin singing. Use hand gestures to indicate.

6   Maintain eye contact as much as possible—looking around the group as they sing, making them all feel part of the action.

7   Be careful of the speed of the song. Make sure that it is not too slow and boring, but not too fast so that they become lost. Watch to see how the children are coping with the speed. If necessary, start again— explaining to the children that "I think we need to sing that song a bit faster/slower, don't we!".

8   Learn from experience—every congregation and group of children is different. You will need to observe what works and what does not work when leading a children's song in your situation. For instance, children can be seated in a group at the front of the church when singing, or they can be seated with their parents — one method may be better than another in your church.

Singing session for children only

Singing a selection of songs with a group of children on their own is quite different from leading children's songs in a church congregation. For one thing, the parents are not present. So the song-leader is not just leading the songs but managing the group of children (who need to be well controlled). The song-leader needs to be confident, dynamic and firm, and it is crucial that they be visible and audible to all the children. If possible, have one regular song-leader who can build a relationship with the group—consistency is beneficial for group management and discipline.

Here are some things for the song-leader to keep in mind:

1   Be organised and well prepared—know the songs you will be singing and their order; have song sheets easily accessible; give the pianist/ guitarist a song list.

2   Be flexible—which doesn't mean disorganised. You may need to change the order of the songs or even omit one during the session, as there are so many variables when you work with children (you cannot predict their mood, level of restlessness, punctuality etc.).

3   Seat the children in a tight group with the song-leader close to the children and near their level (i.e. not standing while everyone else is seated on the floor, unless the group is particularly large). Rapport is far easier if you are close to the children.

4   Eye contact is very important with a group of children and that means looking at all the children and not just those in front of you. Seat children so that they can *all* see you. If they can't see you (or they feel that you can't see them) their attention will wander and they might begin to misbehave (behind your back, as it were!).

5   Variety between active and passive songs is important—some songs are loud and active, while others are quieter. Include a combination and avoid long stretches of inactivity. (You might like to intersperse singing with memory verses or quizzes or other activities.)

6   The singing session should not be too long. It's far better to be short and dynamic, than long and boring. Remember that young children, in particular, have a short concentration span.

7   Song sheets should have big, bold type (written in lower case) on large sheets of cardboard, positioned so that everyone can see. Remember that in a group of young children, the song sheets are only for the adults. A way of helping young children to know the words is to use picture cards.

8   Accompaniment can vary
   • the guitar is good because the guitarist can face the children
   • accompaniment isn't always necessary. Don't avoid singing because you have no accompaniment
   • remember that children can be involved in such a way that they will not notice the absence of accompaniment (e.g. by doing actions, using percussion instruments or clapping)

9   Young children, in particular, enjoy percussion instruments. If they are used, it needs to be well controlled. At least half the children should have an instrument and then swap (in a small group every child could have one). Children can make some instruments themselves, like shakers.

10   When teaching a new song:
   • adults (e.g. Sunday School teachers) should learn it beforehand
   • don't teach a song line by line to young children—you will lose them. It's best if adults sing the song through and the children gradually join in. A longer song could be broken into chunks and maybe only part of the song learnt at one time.
   • older children can be taught in a similar way to adults

Songs can be a great way to teach children about God. But the other great thing is how much they enjoy this learning process. By following a few basic guidelines we can maximise this enjoyment and learning for them.

Sound reinforcement 15

by Steve Williams

If the congregation cannot clearly and distinctly hear what we are singing or playing, then we are doing it in vain. It is, therefore, right and proper for us to be concerned about the technical quality as well as the lyrical and musical content of our ministry. Quality sound reinforcement ought to be a priority for all those involved in the public use of music.

Basic terms

In order to effectively understand the principles of sound reinforcement, it is helpful to define some basic terminology.

- *Sound reinforcement* is best described as pursuing the twin goals of communication and participation by augmenting the sound: to make it louder; to carry it further; to distribute it evenly and clearly. Most amplification which takes place within the context of the local church can best be described as sound reinforcement.

- *Public address* refers mainly to outdoor systems where a signal (either from vocals or instruments) is amplified to cover a large area. It applies to situations where, without the sound system, the voice or instrument would not be heard at all by the majority of the audience. This is usually beyond the scope of a local church's regular activities, so it won't be discussed in any detail.

- *Front of house* refers to the area in front of the 'stage' (in most churches, it is where the congregation sits). It generally means any part of the building other than the 'stage'.

- *Foldback* is the sound which is directed back to the musicians and vocalists, so they can hear the balance, level and mix of the music. The most important feature of foldback is to be able to clearly hear the rhythm section. The actual mix ought to be determined by those who need to hear it, not by what the mix-person wants to hear (see further comments in the section on mixing for the music group).

- *Feedback* is the high-pitched howl or squeal heard when microphones are pointed at speakers or held incorrectly. It can be deafening, painful to the ears and can shatter any atmosphere which has been created by the music or vocals.

The sound system

There are at least seven important parts of any sound system:

1 *Microphones* are the basic means of collecting sound and changing it into an electrical signal capable of being amplified.
2 *Pickups* are the small devices which physically attach to an instrument and convert the sound to a signal which can be amplified.
3 *Direct Injection boxes (DIs)* take a signal from unbalanced line level (auxiliary out level) and converts it to a balanced mic level signal. This has a number of advantages, including the ability to drop the earth if a hum occurs and being able to include instruments as well as vocals being fed down a multicore.
4 *Multicores* are thick cables that run all your mic lines down to the mixing desk and output back to the amplifiers. Treat them with care!
5 *Mixer* is a device designed to take signals from a variety of sources and blend (or 'mix') them together in order to achieve the required balance of instruments and voices. To be a good mix-person requires practice, a good ear and the ability to be a flexible team player.

6 *Amplifier* is the workhorse of the system. Amplifiers take the low-level signal from the mixer and sufficiently increase it to drive a set of speakers. It is absolutely essential that the amplifier does its job well, otherwise distortion will ruin the sound being produced.

7 *Speakers* are designed to reproduce the sound being reinforced. SR speakers differ from hi-fi speakers in that they are able to cope with frequencies very different to those played through the average system. For example, very little speech is reproduced through a home system whereas it is a primary concern within your church. Similarly, foldback wedges (or monitor speakers) are different again in that they need to be able to accentuate the bottom and middle end.

Many churches have a sound system which has been installed using the LAR approach (Looks About Right). Rarely does this work properly. It really is worth the effort to get someone who knows what he or she is talking about to assist you in the selection of equipment suitable for your particular application. The general installation rules include:

- Make sure *balanced* mic lines are run from front to back and vice versa. This minimizes the problems caused by RF interference (like the buzz of light dimmers, CB radios and fluorescent lights). The small difference in installation costs is soon repaid through lack of hassles.
- Make sure that the *mixer* is in an appropriate place such that the mix-person has a clear line of vision between the mixing desk and the stage. Visual contact is essential to effective mixing.
- Make sure that the mix-person is fully conversant with the system (obvious advice, but often overlooked in a crisis).
- A mediocre system often can be upgraded relatively inexpensively and it is usually worth doing when it has been installed using the LAR principle!

Choosing and using a microphone

A good microphone picks up the noise you want and ignores everything that you don't want. You'll never find one which does this perfectly, but some do it a whole lot better than others. When choosing a microphone, keep in mind the purpose for which it is designed. It should have excellent feedback rejection; it should only pick up the intended instrument or voice and disregard all other sounds; it must be sturdy enough to endure church life; it must sound good.

In practical terms, we come down to a choice between a couple of microphones. AKG produce a range of superb microphones at reasonable prices. Two to keep in mind are the AKG D90S (a good all round mic) and the AKG D310 (a slightly better and more expensive one). Both of these mics are suitable for most instruments and do a good job with vocals.

A favourite in the rock industry is the Shure SM58. It looks like an ice cream cone painted battleship grey, is incredibly robust and suits vocalists down to the ground. It is not so suitable for instruments (it boosts bottom end when used close up) and is quite expensive.

In the budget end of the market, Arista produce some copies of the above mics. DM950 is a copy of the AKG D90 and can be quite good for use on a stand. Handling noise is a problem, but it still represents pretty good value. CDM580 is a copy of the Shure SM58 mic. It represents excellent value for money and can be ideal for the church wanting to add a couple of really good quality mics without spending a fortune.

When using a microphone in church, the secret to good sound consists of taking time to set up and tune the system properly and adopting an attitude of co-operative teamwork.

There are some rules of thumb to observe: always keep the blunt end of the microphone pointed away from the speakers; don't cup the basket of the microphone in your hand; don't hold the mic too close to your mouth (no closer than 15 centimetres)..

Tips of the trade

If you play a keyboard, bass, synthesizer or anything electronic, provided it has a line out facility, a DI box makes life incredibly easy. Instead of miking the instrument, its signal goes straight through the DI box into the mixer. DIs come in two different kinds:

1 Passive DIs, which simply consist of a line input, a transformer and a balanced output. They are fairly inexpensive and the output is at MIC level.
2 Active DIs consist of a line input and output, a transformer, some sophisticated electronics, an earth lift and a balanced output. They usually require a 9V battery to operate them and often have a little LED to indicate when the battery is dying. They are more expensive and the output is at LINE level.

Multicores save hours and can actually be made by most enthusiasts. Have a good look around, pick up some good quality cable and have a go! A word of advice: shielded computer cable is most suitable for multicores which are not going to be given a really hard time. Treated carefully, it will give you service for enough time to save up to buy better quality cable.

Practice really is important: be aware that a soundcheck is not a time for band rehearsal. It is a time to set sound levels. The time for rehearsal is before and after the soundcheck. If musicians are aware of this, much frustration will be avoided and your system will yield the very best results.

The art of mixing

A mixing board, desk or console collects all the mic and line level signals (including effects) and mixes them into one signal. It has to cope with a variety of levels, modify them and bring them to the point where they are at a convenient operating level. The mixing desk is the heart of any good sound system.

Most mixing desks, other than very basic ones, include at least some of the following controls:

- *Gain* (or *Input Level* or *Trim*) determines how sensitive the channel is to the incoming signal. For example, a vocalist will need more sensitivity than a kick drum. The gain should be at a level where the peak-level indicator occasionally lights up.
- *Channel EQ* refers to the ability to independently control the tone on each channel. Most mixers have this ability. If there are two EQ knobs, it is known as two-way EQ; three knobs means three-way EQ, and so on. Some mixers may allow you to vary the frequencies which you are adjusting. Practice will help you with these.
- *EQ in/out* refers to the ability to ignore or operate the EQ knobs.
- *Group assigns* are switches which only occur on mixing desks which have groups. If the console is described as 16-4-2, this means that you can assign each channel to any one or more of four subgroups and then overall to the left and right channels. For example, you might group the band on to group 1, a solo instrument onto group 2, the backing vocals onto group 3 and the lead vocal on group 4. This makes it really easy to 'bringup' the band or cut the backing vocals, without having to move more than one or two sliders.
- *Pan control* allows the signal to be assigned to the left channel, the right channel or somewhere in between.
- *PFL/Solo* is a button which allows you to listen through headphones

to each individual channel. PFL means 'Pre-Fader Level' and lets you listen to the channel irrespective of the position of the fader. Solo lets you listen to the channel 'post-fader', so you will need to push up the fader to hear anything.

After mastering these basic controls, you will have begun to see the many factors involved in producing good sound. Mixing is an art, requiring patience, a musical ear and a mind for detail. Practice is irreplaceable, as is conferring with musicians to understand the sound that they are after. The key is to have a co-operative attitude—one which seeks to serve others by producing sounds that are pleasing and meet people's needs.

Why musicians should not write hymns

16

by Tony Payne

I don't think I am particularly old, yet I can still remember the excitement when 'It only takes a spark to get a fire going' was first sung in our church in the 70s. It was but the first of a wave of new music in our small country church. There were moving devotional choruses ('Turn your eyes upon Jesus', 'Spirit of the Living God fall afresh on me'); there were stirring biblical numbers with an Old Testament flavour ('Therefore the redeemed of the Lord shall return clap-clap-clap-clap'); and there were plenty of good ol' gospel numbers (like 'Unto thee O Lord') which were obviously written by people who liked both kinds of music—country and western.

Our country Anglican church was probably ten or thirty years late picking up on the 'new' music, but I can still remember the enthusiasm it engendered, especially among the younger members. The explosion of 'choruses' (as opposed to hymns) which had been mediated to the world largely via the neo-pentecostal movement, had reached us at last.

Since that time, the church music scene has continued to develop. In the last ten years or so, evangelicals have begun to see that we need to write our own contemporary congregational songs[*], rather than rely on the best of

---

[*] In this chapter I am talking about the songs we sing in church—whether you call them hymns, choruses or congregational songs—not about solo pieces, evangelistic items or instrumentals.

what we could glean from the charismatic movement. It has become clear that we need more (many more) congregational songs which are modern, fresh and singable, but which also express biblical ideas in a biblical way.

There has been a resulting burst of creativity among biblically-minded musicians. This has resulted in some good material, most of it being very much better than the songs it has replaced. However, it must be said, that there has also been a fairly large amount of mediocre material. As one surveys the efforts of evangelical songwriters in the last ten years, there are not very many songs which seem destined to last, and pass into widespread Christian usage. There are a good many songs which are sound, and at least do not reflect the errors and woolly-minded lyrics of some other choruses—and this is a good thing. However, in terms of excellent songs that really do their job well, especially with regard to the words, the numbers are not (so far) encouraging.

What is the problem? The problem, I would suggest, is that it is we musicians who are writing the songs. Let me explain what I mean.

We have already seen (thanks to John Woodhouse and David Peterson earlier) that the purpose of music in church is to accompany any or all of the dimensions of our meeting together. Our congregational songs can serve as a vehicle for hearing God speak to us, for us responding to God, and for encouraging one another. The content of the congregational singing is therefore very important. It can mediate the very words of God to us. It can shape and give voice to our response to him. It can be the words by which we exhort one another. In this respect, the content of our singing is every bit as important as the content of the sermon.

The really astonishing thing is that, given the function and potential importance of singing, most of our songwriting is currently being done by people with little or no theological training, and who may or may not be any good with words. It is required of preachers that they may be thoroughly trained in God's word and that they be gifted to teach. However, most of our congregational songs are currently written by musicians, who sometimes lack both of these requirements. It is no wonder, then, that too many of the songs that have been written in the past ten years lack theological insight and effective literary communication. They are usually 'correct' (in that they do not teach heresy), and they avoid some of the sloppy and misleading lyrics of earlier choruses, but they still fail to teach and express God's truth in a way that is memorable and effective in the long term.

In other words, the composition of a congregational song involves two components—the music and the words. The *music* needs to be written by the people with that expertise—that is, musicians who are gifted composers.

The *words* need to be written by people with that expertise—that is, people with a thorough biblical knowledge and insight, who can express these truths in words that work as lyrics.

Most modern church songs (music AND words) are written by people whose first and highest gift is music. This may be because we are subconsciously following the paradigm of contemporary song-writing (the Billy Joel model); I am not sure. What I am sure of is that we need more creative partnerships. We need composers and theological poets to work in tandem, so that the quality of the words matches the quality of the music.

This, of course, is how the classic congregational songs of the past were written. The words were written by theologians/pastors with a literary gift: men like Martin Luther, Isaac Watts, George Herbert, Charles and John Wesley, and John Newton. The music was occasionally written by them. More often, however, the tune was taken from elsewhere.

Let's now look at words and music, and consider what qualities a good congregational song should possess.

The words

The words should come first. If singing has the place in our meetings that we have been suggesting, then at every point the content of the words should be the primary and driving factor behind the song's composition. Content should determine form.

The words need to be written by lyrically-minded people who have a deep and thorough grasp of the Bible. There are certainly plenty of well-trained Bible teachers around. The trick is finding those who have a sensitivity for how words work. With poetry being something of a lost art in our society, these people are not always easy to find. But they must be found and encouraged to develop and utilise their gifts.

There are many different kinds of congregational song waiting to be written. Songs can explain Bible passages or a biblical concept; they can exhort people to godliness or evangelism; they can relate the gospel; they can declare God's character and his mighty deeds; they can give voice to our response to God in prayer, worship and thanksgiving.

Whatever the kind of congregational song that is in view, the words should have the following sorts of characteristics:

- Good song-words *approach the topic at hand,* or the Bible passage that is being expressed, with an understanding of the whole Bible and how it fits together. They reflect the Bible's emphasis and direction, as well as properly understanding the details of the passages in their context.

111

- Good song-words are *memorable and powerful*. They repay repetition, for that is what they will get. Good lyrics disclose a little more each time you sing them (up to a point). They are short on jargon; they avoid cliche. They communicate the old, old story in a strikingly contemporary way.

  Of course, some 'Christian' language is inevitable when we are writing about the cross and Jesus and God. But we can be creative in finding alternatives: 'rescue' for 'salvation', 'trust' for 'faith', and so on.

- Good song-words *work as a lyric*. They utilise the power of language, the sound that the words make as they combine, the rhythm of them, the repetition or contrast of sounds. They avoid forced or trite rhymes. (Rhyme should be used for effect, not as a strait-jacket.) Good song-words develop a theme or idea in a direction that works poetically. Key words and phrases used early in the lyric can be picked up and played with and developed as the words progress.

- Good song-words are *easy to sing*. If you can sing verse 1, then you should be able to sing verses 2, 3 and 4 without hesitation; that is, the number of syllables in each line should be consistent from verse to verse. This is an area of great sloppiness in much contemporary congregational songwriting.

All this may seem somewhat daunting, but it is what we must aim at. If you want to develop your ability as a lyricist, you not only need to deepen your Bible knowledge; you also need to start reading poetry. You might like to start by reading the chapter on poetry in James Sire's book, *The Joy of Reading*. It is a good general introduction.

The words to our congregational songs are too important for them to arise haphazardly out of our personal experiences and hobbyhorses. They need to reflect God's agenda, not ours, and be expressed in powerful, communicative words.

The music

With the words in place (or largely in place), the music can begin to take shape. It should start with and stem from the words, giving expression to the emotions that the words evoke, reinforcing the important words, providing a vehicle that carries the words along and makes them even more memorable.

The process of composition varies enormously from musician to musician, and if a second person is writing the words, there will need to be interaction and refinement throughout the whole process. Usually, the composition process starts with a single musical idea—a rhythm, a melodic line, or a chord progression. One musical idea leads to another, and after these have percolated for a while, a pattern starts to emerge.

Good music for congregational songs should have these sorts of characteristics:

- It should *go somewhere*. It should have a melodic direction and resolve to a suitable conclusion. The shape and character of the melody should reflect the 'shape' of the words. It is helpful sometimes to draw the shape of your melody to see what it is doing, to see if there is enough variation and to see if it has any pattern or direction.

    In classical composition technique, a four-line melody goes something like this:

    Line 1: the main musical idea is introduced;

    Line 2: a repeat or variation or development of line 1, often ending in a modulation;

    Line 3: new material is introduced, often with further modulation or sequences, leading to a climax;

    Line 4: the main idea of line 1 returns, perhaps inverted, and resolving to a suitable cadence.

    This pattern or structure is by no means one that should be slavishly followed (although you will find that a great many songs, ancient and modern, follow some variation of this pattern). Indeed, the words should dictate the shape of the melody. However, I have included the above structure, for those who may not be familiar with it, as an example of a tried and tested musical 'shape' which might serve as a good foundation to build on.

- Like the words, the music should be *memorable*. It should be easy to learn and then stick in the mind. Good music does not need to be complicated.

- The music should be *suitable for communal singing*. This is an obvious point to make, but it can be a hard lesson for many of us to learn, especially when our training and musical influences mostly relate to solo performance. Writing music for communal singing is quite different from writing a song that we will sing ourselves. Good church music should avoid difficult rhythms and intervals. The melody needs to be easy to sing for the vast unmusical majority. It must not be too high (D is the highest note that most people can reach with comfort.) This means that some keys might be easier than others to work in (e.g.

C major and D major are obvious candidates).

All this can be difficult to discipline ourselves to do, especially when we come up with a brilliant musical idea that we really want to use. But for the sake of the church, we must resist the urge to make it too fancy.

- The *introduction* should set the tone and key of the song, introduce the main musical idea (or at least allude to it) and prepare the congregation to start singing (i.e. it is a good idea if the introduction finishes on the note that the congregation will start singing).

- It is worth remembering that the process of musical composition itself has *two components*: *melody and harmony*. It may well be that you are gifted at composing really fine melodies, but aren't so good at arranging them or working out a good harmonic accompaniment. This, too, is an area in which more creative partnerships could be formed.

There is much more that could be said about composing music for church use, and keen musicians would do well to undertake some training in the techniques of composition. *Melodic Writing* by William Lovelock is a helpful book to read on the subject (published by Allans). It is rather formal, and its strictures need not be all followed, but it would serve as a good introduction to aspiring musicians who have had little or no training in composition.

Conclusion

This chapter is headed 'Why musicians should not write hymns'. By now, I hope you can see that what I mean is this: *most* musicians should not write congregational songs…*alone*. There are very few of us indeed who have the gifts to write both music and words, and do a good job of both. We need to form more creative partnerships, and be harder on ourselves, especially with regard to the quality of our words and the communal singability of our music.

There is the challenge which, under God, we must strive to meet.

Copyright and church music 17

by John Booker

What is copyright?

As the word suggests, copyright is the right to protect certain creations again copying. Copyright is a property right which can be dealt with in the same way as most other forms of property. For example, copyright in a work can be sold, licensed or even mortgaged.

In many circumstances, the practical effect of asserting copyright in a work is that the copyright owner is entitled to receive compensation (royalty) for the use of his or her work by someone else.

Copyright originally developed from a desire to reward creative effort, although the creation or work must be more than an idea, theory or a concept — it must be a tangible asset — the law of copyright focuses on the expression of creation.

Copyright law in the UK is governed by the Copyright, Designs and Patents Act 1988 ('the Act'). The Act applies to works created in the United Kingdom and extends protection to copyright works created in certain other countries which, along with the United Kingdom, are members of the Berne Convention.

The Act grants protection to:

• literary works (e.g. books, poems, articles, catalogues)

- dramatic works (e.g. plays, film scripts)
- artistic works (e.g. paintings, drawings, sculptures, photographs)
- musical works (e.g. scores, songs, arrangements)
- films, broadcasts or cable programmes
- sound recordings
- computer programmes
- the typographical arrangement of published editions

Under the Act, copyright protection is automatic. There is no need under United Kingdom law to register copyright ownership with any statutory body. The copyright in a work is initially owned by the creator/composer/author. The Act grants to the copyright owner the exclusive right to deal with the copyright in particular ways, including the right to publish the work, the right to reproduce (copy) and the right to make an adaptation of the work.

The Act extends copyright protection for a work for the period of 50 years after the year in which the creator/composer/author dies. In respect to the typography of a published work, copyright exists for a period of 25 years after the publication of the work. However, if the creator/composer/author is still alive or has not been dead for a period of 50 years or more, then copyright still exists in the original work.

How does copyright apply to musical works?
An owner of copyright in a musical work controls the following uses of the work:

- live performance, broadcast and cable transmission
- publication (distribution of copies to the public)
- reproduction (photocopying, printing, recording, copying by hand)
- arrangement (e.g. cover versions)

Composers usually transfer or assign their rights to certain collecting societies to allow commercial marketing of their works. For example, most composers transfer live performance, broadcast and cable rights in the UK to the Performing Right Society (PRS) which collects royalties on behalf of composers and music publishers. Other rights such as recording or sheet music printing rights are normally sold to a recording company or music publisher.

The need for permission

If you wish to perform, reproduce, play or broadcast a musical work, you will need to obtain the permission of the copyright owner or owners. Unless the copyright has expired, or a special exemption applies, any unauthorised use of the musical work will be an infringement of copyright which could allow the owner to take you to court. The Act gives a copyright owner the right to seek a court order restraining unauthorised use of their musical work and, in some circumstances, damages for any loss suffered as a result of such unauthorised use.

It is most important for churches to understand what copyrights are involved in using items such as printed music or recordings, and to identify the use that the church will be making of the musical works (e.g. performance or copying). This will enable the church to work out what permission must be obtained to legally use the works.

Music and churches

1   Live and public performances

The public performance of copyright musical works requires the payment to PRS of a licence fee.

'In public' includes performances in churches, church halls and any other public gathering. However, PRS does allow a special exemption from the obligation to pay royalties where musical works are performed as part of church worship services. If your church is involved in public performance of musical works outside church services, the best way to ensure that the church is acting legally is to obtain a blanket annual licence from PRS.

Selected venues will be asked to submit details of works performed and they will be contacted by PRS individually.

2   Playing recorded music in public

Where recorded music is played by church groups in public, it must be borne in mind that there are at least two copyright interests involved. These interests are the copyright in the musical work itself and the separate copyright in the sound recording of the musical work.

As playing recording music in public constitutes a public performance, the permission of PRS would be needed with respect to the copyright in the musical work. The permission of a separate collecting society known as Phonographic Performance Ltd (PPL) would be needed with respect to the copyright in the sound recording of the musical work.

However, PPL and PRS does not insist on a licence with respect to the public performance of sound recordings if the sound recording is played by a non-commercial organisation for the advancement of religion, for example before and after a church worship service.

3. Recording church services

Many churches make cassette or video recordings of their meetings for distribution among members of their congregation who are unable to attend the service. Usually such recording includes copyright material, especially music.

Any recording of copyright music must be licensed by the Mechanical Copyright Protection Society (MCPS). They provide a 'Miscellaneous Recordings Licence' for an annual fee. Recording must be limited to non-commercial activity i.e. not for sale through normal retail outlets and limited to a set maximum quantity.

4. Copying printed music

This is probably the most sensitive area of copyright for the reason that the photocopier and overhead projector are wonderfully tools for the infringement of copyright in printed music and lyrics. Perhaps without realising it, many churches are depriving authors of their livelihood by using songs without permission.

As a general rule, all copying (including copying by hand and photocopying) of printed music requires the permission of the owner of the copyright in that work. If the lyrics are printed separately, it may be necessary to obtain additional permission.

There is no collection agency for royalties with respect to the copying of printed music. Legally, there is absolutely no obligation whatsoever on the copyright owner to allow the reproduction of his or her musical score, whether it be in weekly service sheets or onto overhead transparencies. Permission to copy music must be obtained direct from the copyright owner.

5. Copying lyrics

Once again, it should come as no surprise that many songwriters, poets and music publishers get very upset when lyrics are reproduced without permission in leaflets, service sheets or on overhead transparencies. It is a clear infringement of copyright for lyrics to be reproduced without the licence of the copyright owner, thereby depriving the copyright owner of his or her livelihood and the reward for his or her creativity.

Relief is at hand

Having looked at the situation regarding copyright for churches, it can all seem rather complicated and a recipe for a musical co-ordinator's headache. However, in recent times, doing the right things has become much easier. Thankfully, a new collecting society has been established which grants licences to reproduce lyrics for thousands of songs and hymns whether in printed, duplicated or photocopied song sheets and song books, overhead transparencies or weekly service sheets or bulletins. The collecting society operates internationally and its European branch is called Christian Copyright Licensing Ltd (CCL). CCL gives to a church one simple 'blanket' clearance and covers the majority of copyright owners and music publishers of Christian hymns and songs. The cost of the CCL licence is based on the size of the congregation and the annual licence fee ranges from £40 for a church with less than 50 people to £318 for a church with up to 3000 people.

It is recommended that all churches contact CCL to discuss licensing to ensure that no copyright problems arise with respect to the reproduction of lyrics. Not only does the purchase of such a licence ensure that songwriters are properly recommended for their creative effort, but it also provides rights to the lyrics of an enormous number of songs and hymns, over 100,000 from more than 800 copyright owners.

All enquiries concerning licences should be directed to CCL at the following address:

Christian Copyright Licensing Ltd
PO Box 1339
Eastbourne
East Sussex BN21 4YF
England

Tel: (0323) 417711
Fax: (0323) 417722

Part IV :
Checklists

Four handy checklists to
photocopy and keep in
your music folder.

Good leadership

Positives

1. Pray with musicians before and about the church meeting.
2. Be confident in your approach to musicians and the congregation.
3. Communicate clearly what you require from all parties.
4. Introduce songs clearly, being relevant and concise.
5. Use definite arm movements relative to the size of the group.
6. Use regular eye contact and don't be afraid to smile.
7. Build rapport with the congregation and help them relax.
8. Be well-presented, poised and punctual at rehearsals and meetings.
9. Know your words and music well, preferably by heart.
10. Practise your own singing.
11. Stop or restart songs which aren't working.
12. Take control and don't be afraid to lead others—it's your job.
13. Aim to build the musicians into a team who serve each other.
14. Be loving and godly in all your endeavours.

Negatives

1. Don't continually make apologies.
2. Don't attempt to preach during song introductions.
3. Avoid always looking down at the music.
4. Try not to be nervous and uptight—this takes time and practice.
5. Don't be unprepared, or you will be indecisive or flustered.
6. Don't be off-hand—what you say and do matters.
7. Don't set a bad example.

Preparation for music leaders

1. Pray about your song selection.
2. Consult your minister or church leader about the themes and emphases of the meeting for which you are choosing songs.
3. Look for songs suitable for congregational singing and which link up, where possible, with what the meeting will focus on.
4. Consider how songs might fit into brackets (i.e. groups of songs to be sung together).
5. Consider musical links between these songs.
6. Liaise with the person leading the meeting to see if your selections fit into the flow of the meeting. Finalise the song selection and order with the person leading the meeting.
7. Check availability of required equipment.
8. Contact church musicians.
9. Consider the need for teaching or re-teaching songs.
10. Will people stand or sit for songs?
11. Consider how the song's difficulty or the number of songs will affect rehearsal.
12. Rehearse with the church musicians.
13. Consider musicians' seating and orientation.
14. Follow-up the meeting by assessing how things went and where improvements can be made.

Songcheck

1. Are the words theologically correct? Are they not only 'correct' but helpful in their emphasis and approach to the theme?
2. Is the subject of the song worthwhile?
3. Does the song reflect themes or Bible passages from the sermon?
4. Have you obtained copyright permission where required?
5. Is copyright acknowledged on handouts and overheads?
6. Is the song within the technical capabilities of the musicians?
7. Is it in a suitable range and key?
8. Have you considered breath placement?
9. Does the emotional impact of the songs suit their place in the meeting?
10. Do the words and music match up in individual songs?
11. Is there any unusual phrasing or changes that will need to be pointed out?
12. Will any verses or choruses be left out?
13. Do you understand how the structure of the song (its wording and grammar) will affect the vocals?

Suggestions for variety

Styles

1.   Hymns
2.   Modern choruses
3.   Anthems
4.   Items

Presentation

1.   Round
2.   Part singing (male/female; by seating)
3.   Harmonies and descants
4.   Backing vocalists or singing group
5.   Interactive singing
6.   Choral style (soprano, alto, tenor, bass)
7.   Solo (part or all of song)
8.   Modulation (usually up)
9.   Repetition (part or all of song)
10. A capella (no instruments)
11. Tempo (constant or increasing)
12. Rhythm (straight or syncopated or varying)
13. Dynamics (soft or loud)
14. Varied instrumentation between songs and between verses; matching the feel of the song to the instrumentation

Notes